Pocket
HISTORY
of
THEOLOGY

ROGER E. OLSON
and ADAM C. ENGLISH

InterVarsity Press
Downers Grove, Illinois

InterVarsity Press
P.O. Box 1400, Downers Grove, IL 60515-1426
World Wide Web: www.ivpress.com
E-mail: mail@ivpress.com

InterVarsity Press® is the book-publishing division of InterVarsity Christian Fellowship/ USA®, a student movement active on campus at hundreds of universities, colleges and schools of nursing in the United States of America, and a member movement of the International Fellowship of Evangelical Students. For information about local and regional activities, write Public Relations Dept., InterVarsity Christian Fellowship/USA, 6400 Schroeder Rd., P.O. Box 7895, Madison, WI 53707-7895, or visit the IVCF website at <www.intervarsity.org>.

All Scripture quotations, unless otherwise indicated, are taken from the Holy Bible, New International Version®. NIV®. *Copyright* ©*1973, 1978, 1984 by International Bible Society. Used by permission of Zondervan Publishing House. All rights reserved.*

This volume is abridged and revised from The Story of Christian Theology by *Roger E. Olson,* ©*1999 by Roger E. Olson, and published by InterVarsity Press.*

Design: Cindy Kiple

Images: Erich Lessing/Art Resource, NY

ISBN-10: 0-8308-2704-8
ISBN-13: 978-0-8308-2704-6

Printed in the United States of America ∞

Library of Congress Cataloging-in-Publication Data

Olson, Roger E.
    Pocket history of theology / Roger E. Olson and Adam C. English.
        p. cm.
    Includes bibliographical references.
    ISBN 0-8308-2704-8 (pbk.: alk. paper)
    1. Theology, Doctrinal—History. I. English, Adam C., 1974-
II. Title.
    BT21.3.O47 2005
    230'.09—dc22

                                                                          2005018542

P   16   15   14   13   12   11   10   9   8   7   6   5   4   3   2   1

Y   16   15   14   13   12   11   10   09   08   07   06   05

Contents

Abbreviations

AF   Michael W. Holmes, ed. J. B. Lightfoot and J. R. Harmer, trans. *The Apostolic Fathers*, 2nd ed. Grand Rapids, Mich.: Baker, 1989.

ANF   A. Roberts and J. Donaldson, eds. Ante-Nicene Fathers. 10 vols. Buffalo, N.Y.: Christian Literature, 1885-1896. Reprint, Grand Rapids, Mich.: Eerdmans, 1951-1956. Reprint, Peabody, Mass.: Hendrickson, 1994.

NPNF   Philip Schaff and Henry Wace, eds. Nicene and Post-Nicene Fathers, Second Series, vol. 4 (Peabody, Mass.: Hendrickson, 1994).

Act I

A Story Takes Shape

The story of Christian theology does not begin at the beginning. That is, Christian theology began well after Jesus Christ walked the earth with his disciples and even after the last disciple and apostle died. Theology is the church's reflection on the salvation brought by Christ and on the gospel of that salvation proclaimed and explained by the first-century apostles.

The apostles exercised tremendous prestige and authority in the early church. They were firsthand witnesses to the resurrection. While they were alive, their remembrances of Jesus' teachings and deeds were sufficient for the early church's discipleship training needs. When they died, however, Christianity entered a new era for which it was not entirely prepared. It would no longer be possible to settle doctrinal disputes by turning to an apostle. The next generation was compelled to reflect on Jesus' and the apostles' teachings on their own, and thus theology began.

Of course early Christians did not have the luxury of reflecting on their faith in a historical vacuum. Their theology was forged out of debate and struggle. Theological controversy was initially provoked by internal factions *within* Christianity, like Gnosticism, and by opponents from *without*, like the Roman critic Celsus.

GNOSTICISM CHALLENGES THE FAITH FROM WITHIN

The Gnostics did not have a unified organization, and they disagreed among themselves over many issues, but they all believed that they possessed a special spiritual knowledge or wisdom that was greater than that possessed and taught by the bishops and other church leaders of the second century. In a nutshell, they believed that matter, including the body, is an inherently limiting prison or drag on the good soul or spirit of the human person and that the spirit is essentially divine, a "spark of God" dwelling in the tomb of the body. Salvation meant achieving a special kind of knowledge not generally known or even available to ordinary Christians. That *gnosis*, or knowledge, involved awareness of the true heavenly origin of the spirit within. In Gnostic teachings Christ became an immaterial spiritual messenger sent down from the unknown and unknowable God to rescue and bring home the stray sparks of his own being that had become trapped in material bodies.

Some taught that this Christ appeared as Jesus but that Jesus was never really a physical human. This Christology is known as docetism, from the Greek word meaning "to appear" or "to seem." For these Gnostics, Jesus only seemed to be human. Surely God would not taint himself by actually becoming human.

Other Gnostics taught a dualistic Christology in which "Christ" entered into Jesus at the baptism and left him just before he died. He used Jesus' vocal cords, for instance, to teach the disciples but never actually experienced being human.

Many second-century Christians were attracted to this as a special form of Christian truth—higher and better and more spiritual than that taught by the bishops to the unwashed and uneducated masses. Gnosticism appealed to and fostered spiritual elitism, secrecy and division within the budding Christian church.

CELSUS CHALLENGES THE FAITH FROM WITHOUT

While Gnosticism constituted a major internal threat to the church and its apostolic message, early Christian thinkers also had to contend with external challenges from Jewish and pagan writers such as Celsus. Celsus posed a serious challenge to the new faith because he clearly understood that at the heart of Christianity was belief in and worship of Jesus Christ, a man considered to be God in the flesh.

In response to the Christians' worship of Jesus, Celsus wrote: "It cannot be the case that God came down to earth, since in so doing he would have undergone an alteration of his nature."[1] The challenge was simple. Christians claimed to be monotheists—believers in one God—together with Jews and most educated Roman citizens. Yet Christians also claimed that Jesus was God, or at least God's *Logos* (Word, Wisdom), and thus in some sense equal with the heavenly Father and Creator of all things. Celsus believed that this claim about Jesus contradicted the perfection of God's nature as immutable (unchanging). The critique Celsus leveled against the belief in Jesus Christ as God is important to the story of Christian theology because it placed front and center two key questions: Is the Christian God immutable? And in what way is Christ both God and man?

THE APOSTOLIC FATHERS EXPLAIN THE WAY

The apostolic fathers (those who interpreted and applied the apostolic message in the first apostleless generation) were the first to confront the internal and external challenges to the

---

[1]Celsus, *On the True Doctrine: A Discourse Against the Christians,* trans. R. Joseph Hoffman (New York: Oxford University Press, 1987), p. 78.

faith. Persons and writings included in the category of apostolic fathers are Clement, Ignatius, Polycarp, the *Didache (Teaching of the Twelve Apostles)*, *Epistle of Barnabas* and *Shepherd of Hermas*. We will consider only two here: Ignatius of Antioch and the *Shepherd of Hermas*.

Ignatius of Antioch

Ignatius was bishop of the Christians in Antioch—a very important city of the Roman Empire in Syria as well as an important city for Christians. It was there that they were first called Christians, and from there Paul launched his missionary journeys. Ignatius was martyred in Rome around A.D. 110 or 115 and therefore almost certainly knew some of the apostles or at least their immediate successors. He was highly revered and respected by early-second-century Christians, which is perhaps why the Roman authorities arrested and publicly executed him.

It may be fair to say that Ignatius's letters contain the first real Christian theology. Ignatius explored the depth of meaning involved in the Lord's Supper—the Eucharist or Communion ceremony. For him, partaking of the Eucharistic meal constitutes a major aspect of the process of salvation. How does a person become saved and live forever with Jesus Christ? By "breaking one bread, which is *the medicine of immortality.*"[2] Ignatius clearly conceived of the Eucharist (Communion meal) as a sacrament, a means of grace that creates a transformation of the person participating in it. He did not elaborate a theory of this, but he meant to emphasize that by partaking of the bread and wine of the Lord's meal, a person is gaining a participation in divine immortality that overcomes the curse of death brought by sin. Later Christians of both Eastern Orthodox and Roman Catholic persuasions used Ignatius's description of the Eucharist as the "medicine

---

[2]Ignatius *To the Ephesians* 20, in *AF* 151.

of immortality" to justify belief in salvation as a sacramental process of *theosis*—"divinization" or "deification."[3]

On a different level, Ignatius strongly emphasized Christian obedience to bishops. His letters frequently drive home this command: Do nothing without the bishop and regard him as the Lord himself, because "the bishop is nothing less than God's representative to the congregation."[4] To the Ephesians he wrote, "It is obvious, therefore, that we must regard the bishop as the Lord himself."[5] Some commentators see in such statements the beginnings of what has been called the "monarchical episcopacy"—the tendency in later Christianity to elevate the bishop *(episkopos)* to a special spiritual status of power and authority. Certainly Ignatius's sentiment about bishops represents a quantum leap beyond what can be found in the apostles' own writings and no doubt arose from a pressing need to keep order in an increasingly diverse and unruly Christianity.

The Shepherd of Hermas

The other apostolic father to be considered here is the mysterious author of *The Shepherd*. Hermas is especially important in our story because, of all the writings that were considered for inclusion in the New Testament as the canon of Christian Scriptures was being determined, his came closest without finally being included. Various second- and third-century proposals listed *The Shepherd* either as among the inspired books or as part of a secondary group of books to be used as inspirational Christian reading. The great church father Irenaeus of Lyons accepted *The Shepherd* as Scripture, as did third-century fathers Clement of Alexandria and Origen. Even the great Athanasius in the fourth

---

[3]Salvation in such a view, is not merely a one-time decision but a life-long journey toward godliness. As 2 Peter 1:3-4 indicates, the life of godliness means that we "become participants of the divine nature."

[4]Ignatius *To the Romans* 4, in *AF* 81.

[5]Ignatius *To the Ephesians* 6.

century at first accepted it; finally, however, he excluded it. Without doubt, *The Shepherd* of Hermas had great influence among postapostolic Christians in various portions of the Roman Empire, yet it is virtually unknown by most Christians today.

The Shepherd contains a series of visions and their explanations given by an angel to Hermas himself. Many of the interpretations are in parable form and are interspersed with commandments, instructions and mandates for Christian living. The message of *The Shepherd* is that God's mercy is narrowly limited. God will forgive, but not endlessly. Furthermore, forgiveness is conditioned on keeping God's commandments. The Shepherd tells Hermas that "there will be forgiveness for your previous sins if you keep my commandments; in fact, there will be forgiveness for everyone, if they keep my commandments and walk in this purity."[6] Beyond moral purity, Christian belief and practice is a simple affair:

> First of all, believe that God is one, who created all things and set them in order, and made out of what did not exist everything that is, and who contains all things but is himself alone uncontained. Believe in him, therefore, and fear him, and fearing him, be self-controlled. Keep these things, and you will cast off all evil from yourself and will put on every virtue of righteousness and will live to God, if you keep this commandment.[7]

This summary of the gospel not only speaks for Hermas but also summarizes nicely the overall sentiment of the apostolic fathers. While all mention God's mercy in response to true repentance and occasionally express the necessity of God's grace through the cross of Christ, the apostolic fathers seem more concerned with promoting Christian virtue and obedi-

---

[6]*The Shepherd of Hermas* 32, in *AF* 385.
[7]Ibid., 26, p. 375.

ence by instilling fear of judgment for moral failure.

At about the same time that the apostolic fathers were writing to instruct Christians in right belief and conduct, another group of Christians in the Roman Empire was writing letters to pagan critics and Roman authorities, defending the integrity of Christianity against misunderstandings. They also made pleas for an end to persecution of Christians. These writers are known as the apologists.

THE APOLOGISTS DEFEND THE FAITH

The apologists defended the Christian faith by using Greek (or Hellenistic) philosophy to meet their critics on their own terms. They worked to show that Christianity was not irrational or philosophically naive.

Without doubt Justin Martyr (d. A.D. 162) deserves his reputation as "the most important second-century apologist."[8] Very little is known of his pre-Christian life except that he became a philosopher and then became a Christian after a conversation with a mysterious old man. Tradition has it that Justin continued to wear his philosopher's robe after converting to Christianity. It is clear from Justin's writings that he considered himself a Christian philosopher—a philosopher of Christ—just as he had been a philosopher of Plato.

Through his writings Justin explored and explained the concept of Christ as the Logos of God in order to explicate Christian beliefs. For him, this idea—rooted in both Greek and Hebrew thought—was the key to unlocking the mysteries of the Christian gospel. In his account of doctrine, the Logos is God's preexistent Spirit—a second God—who became incarnate in Jesus Christ. Justin was one of the first Christians to explain the Logos and Spirit concept in relation to the Father using the

---

[8]Robert M. Grant, *Greek Apologists of the Second Century* (Philadelphia: Westminster Press, 1988), p. 50.

analogy of fire. The Son's (Logos's) generation from the Father in no way diminishes the Father because, like fire kindled from fire, "that from which many can be kindled is by no means made less, but remains the same."[9] Although Justin did not clearly or completely work out the distinction between the Logos and Spirit as two Persons of the Trinity—a task to be fulfilled by later Christian theologians—he was beginning the process of trinitarian reflection.

As part of his trinitarian musings, Justin claimed that the Logos was in the world before Jesus Christ. The Logos is God's Word spoken through both Jewish prophets and Greek philosophers. Justin identified the *Logos spermatikos,* the "seed of the Logos," as being in every human being and the source of all truth whenever it is understood and uttered. One of the most famous passages in early Christian literature is from Justin's *Second Apology* and expresses his view of the universal, cosmic Logos who is Christ:

> I confess that I both boast and with all my strength strive to be found a Christian; not because the teachings of Plato are different from those of Christ, but because they are not in all respects similar, as neither are those of the others, Stoics, and poets, and historians. For each man spoke well in proportion to the share he had in the spermatic word [logos spermatikos] seeing what was related to it. . . . Whatever things were rightly said among all men, are the property of us Christians. For next to God, we worship and love the Word who is from the unbegotten and ineffable God, since also he became man for our sakes, that, becoming a partaker of our sufferings, He might also bring us healing.[10]

---

[9]Justin *Dialogue with Trypho, a Jew* 128, in ANF 1:264.
[10]Justin *Second Apology* 13, in ANF 1:192-3.

IRENAEUS EXPOSES HERESIES

Christianity's first theologians were the apostolic fathers, and they wrote primarily to exhort, encourage and instruct Christian churches in the transitional time after the deaths of the apostles. Their letters were brief and directed at specific problems. A few of them such as Ignatius of Antioch began to reflect on the meaning of Christian beliefs and practices and add their own words to those of the apostles. The apologists added their voices to the chorus of Christian theology by writing to non-Christian authorities to explain Christian beliefs and practices. In the process they often interpreted them using non-Christian philosophy. Like the apostolic fathers, however, the apologists barely went beneath the surface in exploring and explaining Christian belief as a whole. The apostolic fathers and apologists introduced the setting and plot parameters of Christian theology but did little more. Irenaeus attempted to write the first major chapter of theology's story.

Irenaeus (A.D. 120-202) lived in a time of intense persecution by the Roman Empire against Christians; indeed, he was killed in Lyons during a massacre of Christians. He also lived during a time when Gnosticism was spreading rampantly through the churches. Irenaeus perceived that Christians were in need of education and theological training. Such training in Christianity must start with a richer, more coherent understanding of redemption.

Irenaeus set to work on a deeper conception of redemption, which is known as his "theory of recapitulation," from the Latin term *capitus,* which means "head." *Recapitulatio* literally means "reheading" or "providing a new head." Of course, Irenaeus was not thinking at all of a literal head, as the top part of a body, but of "head" as the source or origin of something, such as the head of a river or stream. The incarnation is an act of recapitulation—Christ not only "sums up" all of humanity, he also provides humanity with a new "head," a new beginning (Eph 1:9-10, 20-23).

Irenaeus sought to show that the gospel of salvation taught by the apostles and handed down from them centers on the incarnation, the human flesh-and-blood existence of the Word, the Son of God. Therefore he emphasized every point of Jesus' life as necessary for salvation. For Irenaeus (and most of the church fathers after him), incarnation itself was redemptive, not merely a necessary step toward either Christ's teachings or the cross event.

The incarnation became, for Irenaeus, the key to the entire history of redemption and to personal salvation. The incarnation itself is transformative, for it began a process of reversing the corruption of sin that results in alienation from God and death. Recapitulation, was Irenaeus's theological expression for how the physical incarnation of the Word in Jesus Christ works to transform humanity. In a literal sense the entire human race is "born again" in the incarnation. It receives a new head—a new source, origin, ground of being—that is unfallen, pure and healthy, victorious and immortal. It is "fully alive," both physically and spiritually.

In the background of this thinking, of course, are Paul's reflections on Adam and Christ in Romans 5. Without some awareness of that all-important passage, it is impossible to grasp what Irenaeus is teaching. His theory of recapitulation is an extended and sustained interpretation of Romans 5. Christ is the second Adam of the human race, and in him "God recapitulated in Himself the ancient formation of man [Adam], that he might kill sin, deprive death of its power, and vivify man and therefore His works are true."[11]

When Irenaeus wrote that in Jesus Christ God "recapitulated the ancient formation of man," he meant that in the incarnation the Word (Logos) took on the very "protoplast" (physical source) of humanity—the body of Adam—and lived the

---

[11]Irenaeus *Against Heresies* 1.11, in ANF 1:448.

reverse of Adam's course of life that resulted in corruption. All of humanity is descended from that protoplast, the first Adam. In order to reverse the Fall and renew the race that fell because of Adam, the Word had to live through it. From Mary, then, the Word took "the very same formation" as Adam—not just one like it. Adam was in some mysterious way reborn of Mary as the humanity of Jesus Christ.

If this is the case, then the real crux of Christ's accomplishment of redemption came at the event of temptation by Satan in the wilderness. When the serpent came to Eve and to Adam, they were conquered and fell. When Satan came to Adam again in Christ, Satan was conquered and put down, and humanity through its connection with Christ achieved a great victory and regained life.

If the temptation was the crux, the cross and resurrection were the culmination of Christ's work of recapitulation. By dying in obedience to God, Jesus Christ provided the ultimate sacrifice and conquered death. Those who willingly participate in Christ's new humanity by choosing him rather than the first Adam as their "head" through repentance, faith and the sacraments receive the transformation made possible by the incarnation of the Son of God. They enter into a new humanity, a new race, with the hope of sharing in God's own immortal, divine nature. For Irenaeus, then, redemption is a process of restoring creation rather than of escaping creation as it was for the Gnostics.

THIRD-CENTURY TENSIONS AND TRANSFORMATIONS
Clement and Tertullian Examine Philosophy

The relationship between philosophy and Christian theology has been a major point of controversy within Christian thought. Clement of Alexandria and Tertullian of Carthage represent opposite ends of the Christian spectrum of thought on the issue. Clement, like Justin, regarded Christianity as the true philosophy that does not contradict or cancel out Greek philosophy but fulfills it. Tertullian vehemently objected, arguing that Christian theology and Greek philosophy were antithetical to each other and should never be mixed.

More than any other early Christian writer, Clement of Alexandria (d. 211/216) valued the integration of Christian faith with the best learning of the day. His motto was "All truth is God's truth wherever it may be found," and he attempted to bring together the stray rays of divine light that he believed were diffused throughout the various philosophical and religious systems, while submitting all to the overriding authority of the Scriptures and the apostolic tradition.

Clement went to the extreme of identifying the ideal Christian as "the true Gnostic" or "the perfect Gnostic." By "true Gnostic," Clement meant a person of wisdom who lives a life of the mind and shuns the lower life of pursuing bodily desires and pleasures. The true Gnostic was imaged by Clement as a Christian Socrates or Plato: a person who stands against the general tendency to "go with the flow" of the confused crowd, reveling at parties and seeking material gain. Such a person seeks to be conversant with all kinds of wisdom and aims to rise above bodily passions, becoming Godlike in virtue and wisdom. Clement went so far as to state that the true Christian Gnostic can "become God" in this life by putting off "desire" and becoming "impassible, free of anger."[12] He made clear that he did *not* mean that the true Gnostic actually becomes perfect in the same way God is perfect. Rather, he meant that such a person puts on the image of God and becomes truly good, although only as a creature dependent on God. Clement had in mind the idea of divinization—that the goal of salvation is to be godly, to share in the divine nature (2 Pet 1) by having the image of God fulfilled and by attaining immortality.

---

[12]Clement *Stromata* 1.22, in ANF 2:437.

For Clement, any achievement of perfection is a work of God that comes about through the human person's yielding to God, shunning the lower life of the body and seeking the higher life of the mind in contemplation and study. The "teacher" throughout this process is Jesus Christ himself, the Word of the Father who "cures the unnatural passions of the soul by means of exhortations."[13]

Tertullian (150-212) was horrified by Clement's overall approach to Christian theology. So disgusted he was at such theological decadence (and the moral decay of the church in general) that he eventually defected from the Great Church and joined the Montanist "New Prophecy" church in Carthage.

Wary of any use of Greek philosophy, Tertullian advised Christians to avoid rationalizing Christian beliefs with Greek philosophical categories. Most scholars agree that he intended to warn against the approach to theology and philosophy taken by Justin Martyr earlier and by Clement of Alexandria in his own time. He famously asks: "What indeed has Athens to do with Jerusalem?"[14] "Athens" refers to the Platonic Academy and by extension to all Greek philosophy. "Jerusalem" refers to the teachings of Jesus and the apostles. While Tertullian did not disallow questioning and seeking *within* Christian faith and belief—that is, within the bounds of apostolic succession and the "apostolic rule of faith"—he did reject any study of nonbiblical, nonapostolic sources to supplement or even interpret the witness to truth that transcends all human inquiry and investigation.

Some of Tertullian's statements about Christian faith and the nature of belief seem fairly extreme. For example, he wrote, "To know nothing in opposition to the rule [of faith] is to know all things."[15] On the surface, at least, this statement makes little or no

---

[13]Clement *The Instructor (Paedagogus)* 1.2, in ANF 2:210.
[14]Tertullian *Prescription Against Heretics* 7, in ANF 3:246.
[15]Ibid., 13, in ANF 3:250.

sense. However, Tertullian was using hyperbole to drive home his point that the most important knowledge is that consistent with and in conformity to the apostolic message. More controversial is his remark regarding Christian belief in the incarnation and death of the Son of God. Controverting other theologians' attempts to explain it speculatively and philosophically, Tertullian burst out, "It is by all means to be believed, because it is absurd," and "The fact is certain, because it is impossible."[16]

In spite of these outbursts of fideism (belief by blind faith), Tertullian made important contributions to the doctrines of the Trinity and the person of Christ. He was the first Christian theologian to confront and reject with great intellectual vigor and clarity the simple view that God has one identity which he can display as Father, Son or Spirit, depending on which mask he wears (often referred to as modalism). If it is true, he declared, then the totality of God died on the cross wearing the mask of the Son. The testimony of Scripture stands against this notion, for surely it is clear that the Father did not die on the cross, only the Son. Against such modalistic naiveté, Tertullian developed a somewhat more complex vision of "organic monotheism." That is, God's "oneness" does not rule out or exclude a kind of multiplicity, just as biological organisms can be "one" and yet made up of interconnected and mutual parts.

According to Tertullian, the God Christians believe in is *one substance and three persons (una substantia, tres personae)*. By *substance* he meant that fundamental ontological beingness that makes something what it is, while by *person* he meant that identity of action that provides distinctness. The basic, underlying idea is "distinction without division."

Origen of Alexandria Leaves a Troubling Legacy
Origen of Alexandria (185/6-254/5), like Clement of Alexan-

---

[16]Tertullian *On the Flesh of Christ* 5, in ANF 3:525.

dria, loved speculation and far surpassed Clement in con-
structing a synthesis of Greek philosophy and biblical wisdom
in a grand system of Christian thought. He became a
renowned scholar who produced approximately eight hundred treatises during his career and attracted even pagan philosophers to his Christian catechetical school. Origen's
illustrious career might have never happened had he succeeded in becoming a Christian martyr as a young man.
When Origen's father was in prison awaiting execution, the
son wanted to turn himself in to the authorities and die with
him. Origen's mother is alleged to have hidden the sixteen-
year-old boy's clothes so that he was unable to leave the
house, and thus she saved his life.

Origen's allegorical interpretation of Scripture. One of the keys
to Origen's method of interpreting Scripture is his distinction
of three levels of meaning in it. The three levels correspond to
the three aspects of the human person: corporeal (bodily),
soulish (rational and ethical) and spiritual (having to do with
salvation in the highest sense).

The bodily meaning of a text is its literal reference, and Origen admitted some things that are useful on that level. For
example, some of the legislation given by God through the
prophets, like the Ten Commandments, is instructive and help-
ful for Christians.

The soulish meaning of a text is its moral significance.
Origen urged that in many cases a biblical story hides an ethical and moral principle beneath the surface of the literal
and historical meaning. Old Testament prohibitions of certain foods really refer to moral practices of not associating
with evil people.

The most important level of meaning in Scripture is the spiritual one, which is also mystical and almost always refers in
cryptic fashion to Christ and the Christian's relationship with
God. The spiritual-mystical meaning is always there—even if

undiscovered and unrecognized—and it is the Christian interpreter's task to strive to uncover it. More often than not, it reveals something about the believer's *theosis,* or divinization, as the ultimate goal of salvation and Christian living.

One of Origen's purposes in allegorical interpretation was to relieve the unbearable pressure put on Christians by skeptics like Celsus, who ridiculed many Old Testament stories as absurd and improper to God. Origen's reply was that passages that seem to describe God in ways unworthy of divine being are not to be taken literally; they are anthropomorphisms or allegories. Of course, what should be highlighted here is not Origen's disregard for the literal meaning of the text but his high regard for the nature of God.

Origen's doctrine of God. Origen's doctrine of God is one of the most highly developed and complex in the history of Christian theology. It is both profound and confusing. Origen attempted to answer the many pagan intellectuals who considered Christian teachings about divinity hopelessly primitive and contradictory. They asked how anyone could believe that the one God of the universe, who created and sustains all things, was born as an infant. Who was running the universe during God's infancy? Of course, Origen was not the first Christian to attempt a reply. But he was one of the first to provide a sustained account of Christian belief about God and Jesus Christ and their relationship that was aimed at defeating such objections. In the process he both cleared and muddied the waters of Christian teaching, so that decades after his death his troubling legacy in this area erupted in the greatest controversy in the history of Christian theology.

The place to begin any attempt to understand Origen's doctrine of God and why it became a troubling legacy for the church is to examine his view of God's nature and attributes. For him, God is Spirit and Mind, simple (uncompounded), incorporeal, immutable and incomprehensible. God is "simple substance" without body, parts or passions.[17]

One of Celsus's main arguments against Christianity was that the incarnation would necessarily introduce imperfection into God. If God "came down" to humans, he necessarily changed—for the worse. But God cannot change in any way, for better or for worse, according to Celsus and all other Greek (especially Platonic) thinkers. Origen refused to back off from either of the two crucial affirmations of Christian doctrine: that God is one and perfect in every way (and he even strengthened this through the use of Platonic philosophy) and that Jesus of Nazareth is God. Indeed, "what belongs to the nature of deity is common to the Father and the Son."[18] So how could he answer the questions and accusations of Celsus?

First, Origen attempted to solve the riddles of the doctrines of God and the incarnation by exploiting to its fullest the concept of the Logos. Second, Origen rejected any real ontological change in divinity, even in the Logos, in the process of becoming incarnate: "For, continuing unchangeable in His essence, He condescends to human affairs by the economy of His providence."[19] Both affirmations became stock in trade of Eastern Christian thought. At the same time, however, both were expressed by Origen in ways that led to very differing interpretations and even heresies and schisms.

Despite his intellectual prowess and fervor of Christian devotion, Origen left a troubling legacy. Certainly, for Origen, reasoning about God and salvation must take place within a commitment of faith, and that includes an acceptance of the truth of the church's tradition and especially the teachings of the apostles. Unfortunately, he ended up unwittingly accepting and teaching some ideas that seem more consistent

---

[17]Origen *De principiis* 1, in ANF 4:245.
[18]Ibid.
[19]Origen *Against Celsus* 4.14, in ANF 4:502.

with pagan philosophy and culture than with the teachings of Moses and other prophets and Paul and other apostles. The church as a whole later judged that this was indeed the case and condemned Origen as a heretic. Nevertheless, in his actual description of the "divine philosophy" of Christian theology, Origen promoted strict adherence to the Scriptures and the apostolic tradition and argued that speculation beyond them is permitted only where it remains consistent with them.

In the final analysis, then, Origen's contribution is a mixture of the positive and the negative. In terms of overall influence he stands alongside Irenaeus before and Augustine afterward. He was in many ways a model of a great Christian intellectual, and he sacrificed his life in service of the faith. On the other hand, his ambiguous teaching about God, Scripture and Jesus Christ left a complicated legacy that would eventually have to be sorted out.

Cyprian of Carthage Promotes Unity

Cyprian of Carthage was born around 200 and served as bishop of Carthage during a very turbulent period in church history, from 248 until his public execution by Roman authorities in 258. At a time of great persecution, strife, schism and heresy within Christianity, Cyprian stepped forward and both taught and lived a style of Christian leadership that became normative for the catholic and orthodox church for a thousand years.

To be specific, Cyprian standardized the role of bishop within the Great Church and made it absolutely central to the ecclesiology (doctrine and life of the church) of catholic and orthodox Christianity. The life and thought of Cyprian is in many ways the answer to the often-asked question, how did the Christian church become Catholic? That is, Cyprian's ideas about the office of bishop greatly contributed to making Christianity both East and West a highly structured spiritual hierarchy.

Of course Cyprian did not invent this Christian ecclesiology (which would better be called "episcopal," after *episkopos,* the Greek word for "bishop"). It was developing long before he appeared on the scene. What was relatively new was his virtual equation of the church itself with the community of bishops. For him, anyone who attempted to live, worship or teach as a Christian apart from the sanction of a duly ordained bishop in apostolic succession was a schismatic and had left the church of Jesus Christ behind. Thus Cyprian was apt to say, "Without the church as mother one cannot have God as father," and "Outside of the church there is no salvation."[20]

Furthermore, Cyprian was one of the first church fathers to clearly and unequivocally affirm baptismal regeneration—the idea that salvation happens at and by water baptism duly administered by an ordained bishop or his authorized agent, the priest. While he attributed all the saving energy to the grace of God, he considered the "laver of saving water" the instrument of God that makes a person "born again," receiving a new life and putting off what he had previously been.[21] Cyprian strongly affirmed that infants are all born guilty of Adam's sin and that the guilt is washed away only by the water of baptism.

Cyprian's writings provide insight into the rapid institutional developments within the church. At the dawn of the fourth century, Christianity was evolving from a relatively disunited underground sect into a highly organized, hierarchical institution. Even so, no one could have guessed that in 312 the new emperor of Rome, Constantine, would convert to Christianity. Further, no one could have guessed the far-reaching impact his conversion would have on the empire and the church. Not only

---

[20]Cyprian *On the Unity of the Church* (Treatise 1) para. 6; *Epistle 72,* para. 21, in ANF 5:423, 384.
[21]Cyprian *Epistle 1, To Donatus* 3-4, in ANF 5:275.

did Emperor Constantine convert, but he legalized Christianity and strongly encouraged all Romans to convert. He perceived that Christianity might be used as a glue to hold together the fragile Roman Empire. But in order to provide the political stability of a common faith, Christianity first needed to find its own doctrinal coherence. If Christianity was to stabilize the empire, it would first need to be stabilized.

Act II

The Plot Thickens

Something truly amazing happened in Alexandria in 318: rioting between Christians broke out in the streets over a point of theology. It all began with an argument between the bishop, Alexander (d. 328), and a popular and ambitious presbyter named Arius (250-336). Ironically, the argument sprang from a belief that Alexander and Arius held in common, namely, that God is ontologically perfect. God would not be God if God were not perfect. This being the case, God can never experience change. For God to change would imply that God lacked something or was in some way deficient. Both Alexander and Arius assumed that if God needed some experience or was benefited by some change, then apparently, God was not initially perfect. Another way to put this point is to ask if God needed to create the world to be God. Does the world add anything to God's perfect being? Theologians typically answer without hesitation that God would be the same God with or without creation.

Absolute static perfection—including *apatheia,* or impassibility (passionlessness)—is essential to the nature of God according to Greek thought, and nearly all Christian theologians came to agree with this. Of course, in the Scriptures they could find several supporting passages that deny change and variability in God. Immutability and impassibility, then, became chief attributes of God in Christian theology. Arius and his followers exploited the argument that if Jesus Christ is the incarnation of the Logos, and if the Logos is divine in the same sense that God the Father is divine, then God's nature would be changed by the experience of human life and death in the form of Jesus. But since it is impossible for God's nature to change, the Logos who became incarnate in Jesus Christ must not be fully divine but rather a great and exalted creature.

One of Arius's duties as a presbyter in Alexandria was to direct the exegetical school, a school of biblical interpretation for priests and lay Christians who wanted to teach. In the course of his lectures, Arius began to accuse the bishop, Alexander, of denying the true humanity of Jesus Christ. Pushing the issue further, he began to teach Alexandrian Christians that the Logos (or Son of God) was a creature and not equal with the Father. He said that a key difference between the Son and the Father was that the latter was eternal and immutable, whereas the former—the Logos—was created before the world and was capable of changing and suffering. He appealed to scriptural passages where the Word of God (Logos) is shown as subject to God and where Jesus Christ is submissive to the Father.

THE COUNCIL OF NICAEA AND ITS FALLOUT

Conflict between Arius and Alexander escalated until the emperor himself heard about it. Emperor Constantine then called on all Christian bishops to gather at Nicaea, his temporary residence while Constantinople was under construction, and resolve the dispute.

Three hundred eighteen bishops arrived in Nicaea in 325 to

attend the first ecumenical council in Christian history. Most probably did not know what to expect. The basic question put before them was: "Is the Logos God in the same way that the Father is God?" After much debate, the council suggested that one way to answer the question and resolve the dispute would be to compose a unifying and compulsory creed, or statement of faith. The Arians and their sympathizers argued strongly for using only biblical wording. Alexander's camp recognized this as a ploy. The Arians had become adept at "Scripture twisting," so that any biblical terminology could be interpreted in their favor. The only way to bring closure to the debate and make clear once for all that the Arian subordination of the Logos to the Father was heretical was to use extrabiblical terminology that clearly spelled out the unity of Father and Son as equal within the Godhead.

After some wrangling and little agreement, the emperor's chaplain Hosius proposed that the new creed include an affirmation that the Son is *homoousios*—consubstantial—with the Father. The compound word *homoousios,* made up of the Greek words for "one" and "substance," was accepted by the majority of bishops to describe the relationship of the Son of God to the Father. They are "one substance" or "one being."

The Arians were horrified. Some non-Arians were mystified and worried. The anti-Arian Trinitarians like Alexander were jubilant.

Emperor Constantine appointed a commission of bishops to write up the creed to be signed by all the bishops, including those who had been unable to attend the council. The result was the first Nicene Creed, which did not include a full article on the Holy Spirit and the church. That would be added later by the second ecumenical council at Constantinople in 381. The Nicene Creed (known also simply as "Nicaea") was patterned after the Apostles' Creed, with added wording to make clear that Arianism is wrong:

We believe in one God, the Father almighty, maker of all things visible and invisible; And in one Lord Jesus Christ, the Son of God, begotten from the Father, only—begotten, that is, from the substance of the Father, God from God, light from light, true God from true God, begotten not made, of one substance [homoousios] with the Father, through Whom all things came into being, things in heaven and things on earth, Who because of us humans and because of our salvation came down and became incarnate, becoming human, suffered and rose again on the third day, ascended to the heavens, and will come to judge the living and the dead; And in the Holy Spirit.[1]

The phrase "begotten not made" is an excellent example of the extrabiblical wording that Alexander insisted was necessary to rule out Arianism. *Begotten* is a biblical word for the Son of God. The Gospel of John uses it frequently. But "not made" is nowhere used in relation to the Son of God in Scripture. The distinction, however, is all-important. If the Son of God is "made" or "created," then he is not truly God. Scripture affirms that he is divine, and salvation requires that he be divine. The bishops gathered at Nicaea recognized that they were affirming a deep mystery, but they were willing to affirm mystery rather than allow heresy. Also found in the middle of the creed is the phrase "of one substance with the Father" to describe the Son of God who became Jesus Christ. That phrase is an English translation of *homoousios* and is simply an updated version of *consubstantial*, which is often found in older English versions of the creed. All in all, the creed shut the door on Arianism. Yet it left the door open to other problems.

---

[1] Justo González, *A History of Christian Thought*, vol. 1, *From the Beginnings to the Council of Chalcedon*, rev. ed. (Nashville: Abingdon, 1992), p. 267.

Attached to the end of the creed was an *anathema,* a brief statement of the heresy being denounced: "But as for those who say, There was [a time] when He [the Son of God] was not, and, before being born He was not, and that He came into existence out of nothing, or who assert that the Son of God is of a different hypostasis or substance, or is created, or is subject to alteration or change—these the Catholic Church anathematizes."[2] Arius was deposed and condemned as a heretic. He was to be exiled together with any bishops who supported him.

ATHANASIUS STUBBORNLY KEEPS THE FAITH

The new Nicene Creed was not a complete victory. When Athanasius (296-373), the "Black Dwarf," succeeded Alexander as bishop of Alexandria at the young age of thirty, trouble was brewing in church and empire. The creed and council had failed to explain the correct distinction between Father and Son and had neglected the Holy Spirit almost altogether.

In 332 Constantine declared Arius restored as presbyter in Alexandria and ordered the new bishop to accept him back into communion there. Athanasius refused unless Arius would affirm *homoousios* as describing the relation between Father and Son. Arius would not. Athanasius rejected him and ignored the emperor's pleas and threats. As a result Athanasius was exiled by Constantine to the farthest outpost of the Roman Empire in the West, the German city of Trier. His exile began in November 335 and lasted until Constantine's death in 337.

Throughout his life, Athanasius valiantly defended the Nicene Creed and the doctrine of *homoousios.* He contended that if the Father is God, then the Son must be God as well, for otherwise the Father would have changed in becoming Father. If there was a time when the Son was not, then there was a time when the Father was not a father. For him, the Son is part of

---

[2]Ibid., pp. 267-68.

the definition of God as Father, and "God's offspring is eternal, for His nature is ever perfect. . . . What is to be said but that, in maintaining 'Once the Son was not,' they rob God of His Word, like plunderers, and openly predicate of Him that He was once without His proper Word and Wisdom, and that the Light was once without radiance, and the Fountain was once barren and dry."[3] For Athanasius, denial of the eternal deity of the Son of God was a serious offense against the Father: "This assault upon the Son makes the blasphemy recoil upon the Father."[4]

For Athanasius, the whole point of theology is to preserve and protect the gospel, and the gospel is about salvation. If the Son of God is not "truly God" in the same sense as the Father, then he cannot save humanity, because only God can undo sin and bring a creature to share in the divine nature. God exchanged God's comfortable robes of deity for the tired, ill-fitting rags of sinful humanity so that we might take off the rags of sin and "put on Christ." It was Athanasius who provided the most famous expression of this "wonderful exchange" theory of salvation: "For He was made man that we might be made God; and He manifested Himself by a body that we might receive the idea of the unseen Father; and He endured the insolence of men that we might inherit immortality."[5]

THE COUNCIL OF CONSTANTINOPLE SETTLES THE ISSUE

When Athanasius died in 373, an Arian emperor was in power, and various forms of Arianism—some moderate and some extreme—were influential among bishops. At least twelve different creeds expressing various kinds of Arianism had been written and promulgated since the Council of Nicaea and Constantine's defection from its accomplishment. None of the rival

---

[3]Athanasius *Four Discourses Against the Arians* 1.14, in NPNF2 4:315.
[4]Ibid., 1.25, in NPNF2 4:320.
[5]Athanasius *On the Incarnation of the Word* 54.3, in NPNF2 4:65.

creeds stuck, but without the arguments and explanations of the Cappadocian fathers, it is possible that eventually an Arian or semi-Arian creed would have been accepted by the majority of bishops and by a powerful emperor, and Christianity would be a different religion from what it is.

Thanks to the work of three great Cappadocian fathers, Basil the Great, Gregory of Nyssa and Gregory of Nazianzus, Arianism did not finally win the day. Here we will consider only Gregory of Nazianzus (329-391), a close friend of the two brothers Basil and Gregory and their sage sister, Macrina. Gregory of Nazianzus became especially critical to the story when he was appointed patriarch of Constantinople, one of the highest positions in the entire church and virtually equal in honor with the bishop of Rome, and was asked in 381 to preside over the council convening at Constantinople. Despite this résumé of important positions, Gregory was no administrator and did not relish his administrative duties. Rather, he was a theologian.

Gregory of Nazianzus was able to sort out two related theological problems. First, his generation struggled with the question of what it means to say God is Three in One. Gregory, together with Basil, helped to resolve the logical contradiction of the Trinity by offering a distinction between *ousia* (substance) and *hypostases* (subsistences). To speak of God's *ousia* (essence, being or substance) is to identify God's general nature—for instance, to say that God is eternal, noncorporeal, uncreated, unlimited. The language of *ousia* answers the question, "*What* are we talking about?" We are talking about one thing, God. But to the question, "*Who* is this God we are talking about?" the church answers, "Father, Son and Spirit." God's singular *ousia* manifests itself in three *hypostases,* or subsistences.

Because the notion of subsistence is obtuse, *hypostasis* is in general rendered more simply as "person." Thus theologians talk about the three Persons of the Godhead. Yet Gregory preferred to think of the three *hypostases* of God not so much as "persons" but as "relations." Within the Trinity itself, he explained, there are not "three beings" but "three relations," and relations are neither substances (beings) nor merely actions (modes of activity). The Father's unique identity within the one divine being is his relatedness to the Son and Spirit as their begetter and source of procession. The Son's unique identity is as the One who is eternally generated from the Father as his express image and agent. The Holy Spirit's unique identity is as the One who eternally proceeds from the Father as his wisdom and power. Each member's identity is defined only in relation to the other members of the Trinity. In other words, Father, Son and Spirit do not possess independent identities, lest such identities constitute them as independent beings. Rather, ontologically speaking, God's one being is composed of three relations, three *hypostases*.

A second question that perplexed Gregory's era involved a new way of understanding the union of Christ's divinity and humanity proposed by a fellow trinitarian theologian named Apollinarius (310-390). Apollinarius wanted very much to emphasize the real deity of Jesus Christ and of the Son of God who became incarnate in him. He set out to explain to his contemporaries, shortly before the Council of Constantinople, how it is that Jesus Christ could be both *truly human* and *truly divine*—of one being *(homoousios)* with both God and humans.

Apollinarius starts with the assumption that human persons are composed of three distinct and even separable aspects: body, soul and rational soul, or spirit. This tripartite composition of humanity is borrowed more from Platonic philosophy than from Scripture, even though the New Testament does mention all three aspects.

Apollinarius went much further than the New Testament by directly identifying the body or physical nature as the lower nature and the rational soul or spirit as the higher nature. The soul is the animating life force that exists in nonhuman creatures as well as in humans. It is part of the lower nature. According to Apollinarius, Jesus Christ was divine in that the eternal Logos—Son of God—took the place of a rational soul in him. His body and animating soul (life force) were human, but his spirit (mind, consciousness) was not; it was divine. The impression given by this Christology is of "God in a bod"—an omniscient being inhabiting a creaturely body and using it as a vehicle without actually becoming human and experiencing human limitations and sufferings. Of course, one of Apollinarius's motives was to show how Jesus Christ could be God (immutable, impassible, omniscient) and human (limited, finite, suffering, mortal) at the same time. He did not think he was inventing any new idea. He thought he was just packaging Origen's and Athanasius's Christologies in a better way. He may have been right.

Gregory of Nazianzus, who presided over the Council of Constantinople, intuited that if Jesus Christ's humanity was not complete humanity, then our human nature cannot be wholly saved through it. The way Gregory expressed this was by the formula "What has not been assumed has not been healed."[6] In other words, if Jesus' humanity was not a whole human nature—body, soul and spirit—then the "wonderful exchange" could not work. The divine Son of God had to have joined his divine nature with a whole human nature—everything essential to being human—in order to heal or restore it. That part that was not human in him would not be healed in us. For Gregory, then, Apollinarianism undermined salvation itself and had to be rejected.

The Council of Constantinople, under the guidance of Gregory of Nazianzus, repudiated all Apollinarian proposals

---

[6]Gregory of Nazianzus *Letter 101,* quoted in Anthony Meredith, *The Cappadocians* (Crestwood, N.Y.: St. Vladimir's Seminary Press, 1995), p. 44.

and clarified the orthodox understanding of incarnation. Furthermore, the council reworked the Nicene Creed so as to make it fully trinitarian and thus avoid either the suggestion that the Holy Spirit is less than or subordinate to the Father or the suggestion that Father, Son and Spirit are simply modes or forms that the one God can take depending on the need. The revised Nicene Creed, also known as the Niceno-Constantinople Creed, reads:

> We believe in one God,
> the Father, the Almighty,
> maker of heaven and earth,
> of all that is, seen and unseen.

> We believe in one Lord, Jesus Christ,
> the only Son of God,
> eternally begotten of the Father,
> God from God, Light from Light,
> true God from true God,
> begotten, not made,
> of one Being with the Father.
> Through him all things were made.
> For us men and for our salvation
> he came down from heaven;
> by the power of the Holy Spirit
> he became incarnate from the Virgin Mary,
> and was made man.
> For our sake he was crucified under Pontius Pilate;
> he suffered death and was buried.
> On the third day he rose again
> in accordance with the Scriptures;
> he ascended into heaven
> and is seated at the right hand of the Father.
> He will come again in glory to judge the living
>   and the dead,

and his kingdom will have no end.

We believe in the Holy Spirit,
the Lord, the giver of life,
who proceeds from the Father (and the Son).
With the Father and the Son he is worshipped and
    glorified.
He has spoken through the Prophets.
We believe in one holy, catholic and apostolic Church.
We acknowledge one baptism for the forgiveness of sins.
We look for the resurrection of the dead,
and the life of the world to come. Amen.[7]

The Nicene Creed became the basic universal statement of faith binding on all Christian clergy by decree of the emperor Theodosius and was reaffirmed by the fourth ecumenical council at Chalcedon in 451. Other creeds and confessions of faith were written later, but all of them in the Orthodox, Catholic and magisterial, or mainline, Protestant traditions are meant to be elaborations and interpretations of this one. It is the universal creed of Christendom.

THE CONFLICT IS REBORN

One positive result of the Council of Constantinople and its revised Nicene creed was that it effectively settled the question of the Trinity. From this council on, all Christians were expected to believe and confess God as a single divine being eternally existing as three distinct subsistences or persons. No one who dared question the equal divine dignity and glory of the three Persons as one being had any serious chance of being a church leader. The council also declared that true Christian orthodoxy necessarily includes belief that Jesus Christ was and is both truly

---

[7]Gerald Bray, *Creeds, Councils and Christ* (Downers Grove, Ill.: Inter-Varsity Press, 1984), pp. 206-7.

God and truly human, consubstantial with both God the Father and humans.

Unfortunately, left unclear was *how* divinity and humanity unite in one man. Soon the bishops and theologians of Alexandria and Antioch and their followers throughout the empire were at one another's throat over the nature of the union of the God-man. All agreed that Jesus Christ was God incarnate. The confession itself was not in debate. The question after the Council of Constantinople became, how should Christians explain and express Jesus Christ's humanity and divinity?

Alexandrians and Antiochenes answered the question in two totally different ways. Alexandrians argued that just as the Trinity is one substance, or nature, and three Persons, so Jesus Christ is one nature and one Person. In him the natures of God and humanity join so integrally that they form a compound or hybrid. The Antiochenes argued that Jesus Christ is two natures and two persons who can also be conceived as one Person, just as many communities or societies of more than one person are corporate persons in the eyes of the law. When it comes to personhood, Antiochenes averred, two can become one while remaining two.

NESTORIUS AND CYRIL BRING THE CONTROVERSY TO A HEAD

The tension escalated in 428 when Nestorius (d. 450), an Antiochene, was appointed to the enviable position of bishop of Constantinople by the emperor. Little is know about Nestorius's life, but it is clear that he was a firm proponent of the Antiochene "two natures" interpretation of the incarnation—Jesus Christ was a conjunction of divine nature and human nature: eternal divine Logos and human person Jesus in close union. Alexandrians could not bear to see Nestorius go unchallenged. Cyril (d. 444), bishop at Alexandria, who always had his eye on the coveted post of bishop at Constantinople, spearheaded the attack by entering a correspondence debate with Nestorius.

Nestorius got himself into trouble when, in answering some of Cyril's letters, he attempted to explain the conjunction idea of the incarnation. Cyril knew that if he could get Nestorius to keep attempting to explain it, he would eventually reveal it for what it was—a sophisticated form of adoptionism (in which the body of the man Jesus was merely adopted by the divine Logos). The key similarity lay in the fact that in both Nestorianism and adoptionism the Son of God never actually enters into human existence. The human person in the Nestorian conjunction remains not only distinct in nature but also a different person from the Son of God. Nestorius tipped his true hand when he used the analogy of marriage. He apparently argued that just as two independent persons come together to form a union transcending their differences in marriage, so in the incarnation the Son of God and the Son of David formed a union (initiated by the Son of God) that transcended their different natures. Of course, he said, that union was a bond of fellowship and cooperation of wills that is stronger than any human friendship or marriage.

There is no doubt that Nestorius's intentions were sound. He wished to preserve the integrity of God's nature and human nature even in the incarnation by positing a "union of natures." He wanted also to do full justice to the humanity of Jesus Christ and not allow it to be swallowed up in the divinity or made less than like ours. Yet in spite of his laudable intentions—many of which were shared by more orthodox Christians—Nestorius could not account for the unity of Christ. In the divine-human marriage, the human Jesus was born, educated, tempted, killed and raised, while the divine Christ performed the miracles, revealed the wisdom of God and saved humanity. In the end, in spite of Nestorius's valiant attempt to explain how a conjunction of two persons could count as one person, his Christ turns out to be two individuals and not one. The Son of God did not truly experience human existence "in the flesh" but only "through association with the man." Cyril was right to criticize Nestorius's Christology as little more than a dressed-up adoptionism.

Cyril proposed as a resolution to Nestorius's dilemmas the doctrine of the *hypostatic union*. This becomes the Great Church's foundation for explaining and expressing the mystery of the incarnation of God in Christ. In a nutshell, it means that the subject of the life of Jesus Christ was the Son of God, who took on himself a human nature and existence while remaining truly divine. In other words, according to Cyril, there was no human personal subject in the incarnation. The *hypostasis* (personal subsistence) of Jesus Christ was the eternal Son of God who condescended to take human flesh through Mary. Mary, Cyril argued, gave birth to God in flesh. That is the essence of the incarnation.

Cyril's favorite formula for expressing the incarnation was "God the Logos did not come into a man, but he 'truly' became man, while remaining God."[8] Cyril completely rejected the "conjunction" idea of union and replaced it with hypostatic union—union of two realities in one *hypostasis* or personal subject, the Logos. For him, the Nestorian conjunction idea amounted to little more than a cooperation between two persons, one human and one divine. That could be true of any prophet. Nestorius's views were ultimately adoptionistic. So strong was the union of humanity and divinity in the one *hypostasis* of the Logos, Cyril argued, that one must speak of "one nature after the union." In other words, even though it is possible conceptually to think of Christ's humanity and divinity as two distinct *physeis*, or natures, in reality their union in the incarnation made them to become "one nature."

---

[8]Aloys Grillmeier, *Christ in Christian Tradition*, vol. 1, *From the Apostolic Age to Chalcedon (451)*, 2nd rev. ed., trans. John Bowden (Atlanta: John Knox, 1975), p. 477.

THE COUNCIL OF EPHESUS

In 431, a council was called to meet in Ephesus to resolve the matter. Cyril and his loyal bishops arrived first and waited for a few days. When no one else showed up, Cyril—the only patriarch present—called the council to order and began the proceedings in the absence of Nestorius or any other bishops loyal to Antioch. The bishops voted to endorse Cyril's understanding of the incarnation as the true and authoritative interpretation of the Nicene Creed as it pertains to the person of Jesus Christ. Then the council condemned Nestorius and his Christology as heresy.

Shortly after the Council of Ephesus led by Cyril completed its work, the bishop of Antioch and his colleagues arrived. They immediately withdrew from the bishops already assembled and held a rival council at Ephesus. They proceeded to condemn Cyril and his formulas and reconfirm Nestorius as patriarch of Constantinople. Before they finished, the bishops of the West and papal delegates arrived from Rome and joined Cyril and his council, which quickly ratified the earlier acts condemning and deposing Nestorius. It was all very confusing and ultimately up to the emperor to sort out.

When word of the schism reached the emperor, he strongly pressured the parties to compromise. He supported the council's deposition and exile of Nestorius on the condition that Cyril agreed to affirm the two-natures formula for orthodox Christology. Cyril reluctantly agreed so long as the two natures in Christ were not conceived as divided. For him, "a *distinction* of the natures is necessary, a *division* is reprehensible. To speak of *duo physeis* [two natures] makes a distinction, but does not of itself divide; it only has the latter effect if a reprehensible intention to divide is associated with it."[9]

Cyril clearly preferred the "one nature after the union" for-

---

[9]Ibid., p. 479.

mula, and many of his Alexandrian colleagues and followers were dismayed by his compromise. They felt he had given away the farm, so to speak, by allowing any talk of two natures in Christ. After all, they argued, does not two natures imply two persons? Cyril defended his compromise with Antioch in a document known in church history as the Formula of Reunion by insisting that the two natures are distinct only in thought and not in reality. It is highly unlikely that the Antiochenes agreed. For them the distinction of Christ's two natures was ontological and not merely mental.

The Formula of Reunion of 433 was signed by the bishops of Alexandria and of Antioch and ratified by the emperor. It avoided total schism between the two great cities. Each side got some of what it wanted. Alexandria saw Nestorius condemned and sent into exile, from which he never returned in spite of many efforts on his behalf. Antioch saw Alexandria affirm the incarnation as a union of two natures. However, the Council of Ephesus and the Formula of Reunion proved to be only temporary settlements.

THE CONTROVERSY CONTINUES AFTER EPHESUS

Cyril's successor as bishop and patriarch of Alexandria was a rascal named Dioscorus. Few men in church history have been as universally disdained and scorned as this character. Dioscorus sought to lure the Antiochenes into resuming the debate over the natures of Christ. He hoped that a renewed controversy would prompt the calling of another ecumenical council. His bait was Eutyches, a somewhat feeble-minded but influential elderly monk of Constantinople. Eutyches was a strong supporter of the Alexandrian cause, and after Cyril's death, he sided with Dioscorus regarding the one nature of Christ. What is clear is that Eutyches went a step beyond the language of Cyril and affirmed of the process of incarnation that it involved "two natures *before* the union (of God and humanity) but only one

nature *after* or as a result of the union." He seems to have
taught that right from the moment of conception in Mary, Jesus
Christ was a hybrid of humanity and divinity—a single divine-
human nature—that mixed together and mingled the two
natures so that the human nature was overwhelmed and swallowed up by the divine. "If this were true, then how was he really
our mediator?" critics asked. How could he go through that
process of undoing the fall of Adam and recapitulating the
human race about which Irenaeus spoke so eloquently? How
could his death on the cross represent humanity?

In 448 Dioscorus manipulated a synod of bishops in Constantinople to condemn Eutyches. His reason for bringing
about Eutyches' condemnation was to offer the Constantinop-
olitan monk refuge and fellowship in Alexandria and then use
his condemnation and subsequent communion with Alexandria to force a confrontation with Antioch's leaders and even
with the patriarch of Constantinople himself.

Dioscorus got his wish for a new council, convened at Ephesus in 449. But instead of being the fourth ecumenical council
of Christendom, it has come to be known as the Robber Synod.
Dioscorus arrived with a gang of heavily armed monks and
quickly took control of the entire council. Eutyches' formula
"two natures before the union; one nature after the union" was
approved as orthodox, and the leading Antiochene representative, Theodoret of Cyrus, and other so-called Nestorianizers
were condemned as "contenders with God" and deposed from
their positions as church leaders. Some of the Alexandrian
bishops and many of the monks present called for them to be
burned. Worst of all, perhaps, Patriarch Flavian of Constantinople arrived at the council with a document from Bishop Leo
of Rome against Eutyches. The epistle has come to be known
in church history as *Leo's Tome* and later played a very important role in the solution and settlement of this most unfortu-
nate doctrinal conflict. Pope Leo I—perhaps the first bishop of

Rome to actually function as a pope, in that he virtually ruled
much of Italy as well as all of the Western Church—had sent a
lengthy doctrinal epistle to Flavian condemning Eutyches and
charting out orthodox Christology. Flavian tried to read the letter from the pope, but Dioscorus's monks attacked and beat
him so badly that he died shortly afterward.

At the end of the Robber Synod in Ephesus, "the Bishop of
Alexandria had every reason to be satisfied with the results of
his attack against the doctrine of the school of Antioch."[10] Sens-
ing the shift in momentum, Emperor Theodosius II switched
allegiance from Antioch to Alexandria and fully supported the
acts of the synod. For a time it stood as the fourth ecumenical
council, Ephesus II. The Alexandrian victory seemed complete.
Eutychianism triumphed. However, on July 28, 450, Emperor
Theodosius II died in a freak accident when he was thrown
from his horse.

THE COUNCIL OF CHALCEDON AND THE CHALCEDONIAN DEFINITION

Theodosius's sister and successor, Pulcheria, along with her
consort, Marcian, immediately began a process of reversing the
terrible acts of the Robber Synod of 449. They had Flavian's
body brought to Constantinople from Ephesus and buried with
full honors in the great cathedral of Hagia Sophia (Holy Wisdom), which stood at the center of the capital city. A new council to replace Ephesus II as fourth ecumenical council was
called to meet at Chalcedon near Constantinople in May 451.
All bishops of the Great Church of Christendom were ordered
to attend, and *Leo's Tome* was circulated to them in advance of
the meeting. Leo himself did not attend the Council of Chalcedon because it was not held in the West.

---

[10]R. V. Sellers, *The Council of Chalcedon: A Historical and Doctrinal Survey*
(London: SPCK, 1961), p. 87.

The great ecumenical Council of Chalcedon opened with pomp and circumstance on October 8, 451, with five hundred bishops and eighteen high state officials, including the imperial couple, in attendance. The followers of Leo and the Antiochenes sat on one side of the great hall, and Dioscorus and his cohorts sat on the other side. Only the imperial power could get them inside the same building and keep them there. One of the first events of the first session of the council was the entrance of Theodoret of Cyrus, who had been condemned, deposed and nearly burned by the Robber Synod. A near riot ensued, but the empress and her guards quieted down the bishops and Theodoret was seated in honor. Then the acts of the Ephesian Robber Synod were read aloud and discussed. Gradually Dioscorus's supporters abandoned him and the Robber Synod and expressed remorse for their participation in the persecution of Theodoret and death of Flavian. Only Dioscorus stood defiantly for the validity of what had happened at Ephesus in 449 and defended its actions. At nightfall the bishops voted to depose Dioscorus as patriarch of Alexandria and exile him together with the ringleaders of the infamous Ephesian synod.

Leo's Tome was read aloud and discussed over several sessions. After much debate, a new formulary of faith was agreed upon, based heavily on language and concepts in *Leo's Tome* and Cyril's letters to Nestorius and John of Antioch. The bishops wanted to make absolutely clear that the new Formulary of Chalcedon (more often known as the Definition of Chalcedon) was not a new creed but an interpretation and elaboration of the Nicene Creed of 381. It was finally approved and signed by the emperor and bishops on October 25, 451. The heart of the statement says:

> In agreement, therefore, with the holy fathers we all unanimously teach that we should confess that our Lord Jesus Christ is one and the same Son; the same perfect in

Godhead and the same perfect in manhood, truly God and truly man, the same of a rational soul and body; consubstantial with the Father in Godhead and the same consubstantial with us in manhood; like us in all things except sin; begotten of the Father before all ages as regards his Godhead and in the last days the same, for us and for our salvation, begotten of the Virgin Mary the *Theotokos* [God-bearer] as regards his manhood; one and the same Christ, Son, Lord, only-begotten, made known in two natures without confusion, without change, without division, without separation; the difference of the natures being by no means removed because of the union but the property of each nature being preserved and coalescing in one person *[prosopon]* and one *hypostasis,* not parted or divided into two persons but one and the same Son, only-begotten, divine Word, the Lord Jesus Christ; as the prophets of old and Jesus Christ himself have taught us about him, and the creed of our fathers has handed down.[11]

The real heart of the Chalcedonian Definition is what is known as the four fences of Chalcedon: "without confusion, without change, without division, without separation." These four phrases serve as "fences" around the mystery of the hypostatic union—Christ's two full and complete natures in one person. "Without confusion" and "without change" protect the mystery from the heresy of Eutychianism, which tries to preserve the unity of person by creating a hybrid—*tertium quid* (third something)—out of divinity and humanity. "Without division" and "without separation" protect the mystery from the heresy of Nestorianism, which tries to emphasize the distinction between the humanity and divinity by tearing them apart into two different persons. The definition says: So long as you

---

[11]Bray, *Creeds,* p. 162.

do not violate one of these fences, you may express the mystery of the incarnation in many different ways. The definition does not try to reduce the mystery, but to protect it.

Chalcedon brought resolution to the great controversy between Antioch and Alexandria. This is not to say that it ended all discussion over the natures, personhood, and will or wills of Christ. Indeed, the East carried on the debate for over two hundred more years, resulting in two more councils at Constantinople. In the West, however, the church's attention was being diverted away from christological controversies and redirected toward new and different challenges.

Act III

The Story Divides

Augustine's life (354-430) is the best known of all early church fathers' lives. In fact, we know more about Augustine's personal life than about almost any other ancient person's. That is because he wrote one of the first fairly reliable and detailed autobiographies, known as his *Confessions*. Although it is written in the form of a prayer to recount his spiritual journey and give thanks to God, Augustine's *Confessions* reveals a great deal about his childhood, family, youth, early struggles, mental and physical health, conversion, theological development and life as a leading churchman in North Africa (he became bishop at Hippo). Augustine hid little or nothing from his readers. He laid out in intimate detail his sins from infancy to adult life and yet emphasized at every point the power of God's grace to heal and transform.

AUGUSTINE CONFESSES GOD'S GLORY AND HUMAN DEPRAVITY

Some have labeled Augustine's distinctive style of theology Augustinianism and identified its main feature as "emphasis on the absolute supremacy of God and the accompanying absolute helplessness and dependency of the human soul on the grace of God."[1]

This core of Augustine's theology was not entirely new with him, of course. Church fathers before him also believed in and taught God's supremacy and the human soul's dependency on grace. But Augustine put a new spin on these ideas and linked them together in a new way. Augustinianism introduced into the stream of Christian thought something called monergism, the belief that human agency is entirely passive and God's agency is all-determining in both universal history and individual salvation. Many people today know a part of this as "predestination" and automatically link it with the sixteenth-century Protestant Reformer John Calvin. However, the broader perspective is Augustine's monergistic ideas of providence and salvation in which God is the sole active agent and energy while humans, both collectively and individually, are tools and instruments of God's grace or wrath.

It is important to understand that Augustine's monergism is a reactionary theology. His understanding of grace, salvation and the effects of sin were formulated in reaction to the writings of Pelagius. It is not surprising, then, that his ideas on those topics are sometimes communicated in very sharp language. In the same way, Augustine's theodicy (his beliefs about the problem of evil and the nature of good and evil) and ecclesiology (his theology of the church) were formed in response to two other controversies, Manichaeism and Donatism respectively.

THE PELAGIAN PROBLEM

From his own conversion on, Augustine tended to place great emphasis on the grace and power of God in salvation. It

---

[1]T. Kermit Scott, *Augustine: His Thought in Context* (Mahwah, N.J.: Paulist, 1995), p. 153.

seemed to him that God's action in his own experience of conversion was so overwhelming that he could not really resist it. He did not choose God; God chose him. He believed that this impression was confirmed by the apostle Paul's teaching in passages such as Romans 9—11. In the *Confessions* he praised and thanked God for sovereignly changing him; Augustine gave all the glory to God and conversely acknowledged his own helplessness to do anything good: "My whole hope is exclusively in your very great mercy. Grant what you command, and command what you will. You require continence. A certain writer has said (Wisd. 8:21): 'As I knew that no one can be continent except God grants it, and this very thing is part of wisdom, to know whose gift this is.'"[2]

When the British monk Pelagius (d. 420) arrived in Rome sometime around 405, he noticed that many Christians were living morally indecent lives, while many others seemed unconcerned about this growing indifference to moral purity and obedience in the church. He began inquiring about the possible causes of this, and when he heard or read Augustine's prayer quoted above, he was horrified and immediately sure that this was the root cause of the problem. If Christians became convinced that they could not be continent (to abstain from immorality) unless God gave them that gift, then it should not surprise anyone if they practiced incontinence. That was Pelagius's argument. Pelagius then composed *On Nature,* a book that condemned Augustine's view and argued that humans can live sinless lives through their "natural endowments" and are responsible to do so. This was the catalyst that set off a great controversy over original sin, free will and grace that consumed the Western Church off and on for over a hundred years and echoes down through the subsequent centuries.

---

[2]Augustine *Confessions,* trans. Henry Chadwick (New York: Oxford University Press, 1991), p. 202.

AUGUSTINE'S RESPONSE TO PELAGIUS

Pelagius's opponents, led by Augustine, accused him of three heresies. First, they claimed that he denied original sin. Second, they charged him with denying that God's grace is essential for salvation—and indeed, it seems that Pelagius affirmed the power of free will to assist in the initiation and fulfillment of salvation. Third, they said that he preached sinless perfection through free will apart from grace. In other words, he denied that perfect obedience to God's law is absolutely impossible for fallen humans. There is truth in all three accusations so far as we can tell.

Augustine's entire soteriology (or doctrine of salvation) flows from two major beliefs: the absolute and total depravity of human beings after the Fall and the absolute and total power and sovereignty of God. The way Augustine interpreted these doctrines both developed out of and conditioned his debate with Pelagius and his more moderate defenders, the so-called Semi-Pelagians. Augustine's view of original sin and human depravity is as strong as any can possibly be. According to him, all humans alive at any given time (with the sole exception of the God-man, Jesus Christ) are included in a "mass of perdition" and are altogether guilty and damned by God on account of Adam's primal sin. As the Puritans phrased it in the seventeenth century: "In Adam's fall we sinned all."

Contrary to Pelagius and most theologians of the Eastern churches, Augustine believed that all humans except Christ himself are born not only corrupt, so that sin is inevitable, but also guilty of Adam's sin. All deserve eternal damnation unless they are baptized for the remission of sins and continue in that grace through faith and love.

Because of the inherited depravity and corruption of sin, Augustine argued, fallen humans are not free not to sin. "A man's free will," he wrote against Pelagius, "avails for nothing

except to sin."[3] Before Adam's disobedience, he had the power
not to sin. His condition then was *posse non peccare:* it was possible not to sin. After the disobedience and because of it, Adam's
condition and that of all his posterity except Jesus Christ
became *non posse non peccare:* not possible not to sin.

In spite of the inherited guilt of original sin and the inevita-
bility of sinning, God's plans are not thwarted and his will is still
done: "For the Almighty [God] sets in motion even in the
innermost hearts of men the movement of their will, so that He
does through their agency whatsoever He wishes to perform
through them."[4] In other words, for Augustine God alone is the
all-determining reality, and whatever happens, including
human sins, must be rooted in his sovereign will and power. In
order for humans to be responsible, they must have free will in
their sinning. But in order for God to be sovereign, every event
must be under his control, for "if we maintain that the will of a
human being is not in God's power but is controlled wholly by
the person, then it is possible for God to be frustrated. And that
is just absurd."[5] The only solution is to define free will as doing
what one wants to do. But for Augustine God is the source of
those wants. In whatever happens God's will is being done.

Grace then is absolutely necessary for any truly good deci-
sions or actions of any fallen human person. Augustine argued
this against Pelagius and his followers on several counts. First,
humans are so utterly depraved that unless God gives them the
gift of faith by grace, they would never even think to do anything good. In his own words, "The Spirit of grace, therefore,
causes us to have faith, in order that through faith we may, on
praying for it, obtain the ability to do what we are commanded.
On this account the apostle himself constantly puts faith before

---

[3]Augustine *On the Spirit and the Letter* 5, in NPNF 5:84.
[4]Augustine *On Grace and Free Will* 41, in NPNF 5:462.
[5]Scott, *Augustine,* p. 162.

the law; since we are not able to do what the law commands unless we obtain strength to do it by the prayer of faith."[6] Any other view, he argued, would weaken belief in our depravity and in the sole sufficiency of God's grace, including Christ's death on the cross. That is his second reason for insisting that grace is the sole cause of anything truly good that we do. If anyone could obtain some measure of righteousness by nature and free will alone, apart from supernatural assisting grace, then Christ died in vain: "If, however, Christ did not die in vain, then human nature cannot by any means be justified and redeemed from God's most righteous wrath—in a word, from punishment—except by faith and the sacrament of the blood of Christ."[7]

After Augustine's death, there ensued a great debate over his strict monergism. The Great Church in the West agreed with his criticisms of Pelagius, but many disagreed with his rigid views on sovereignty, election and free will. At the Synod of Orange (in what is now France) in 529, the church took a mediating and somewhat inconsistent position. It condemned Pelagianism even in its modified form, but it did not fully endorse Augustinianism.

POPE GREGORY'S MEDIATION

The figure who largely resolved these issues for the medieval church was Pope Gregory I, also known as Gregory the Great (540-604). Gregory was one of the most important popes and theologians in the history of the Roman Catholic tradition and a major contributor—unwittingly—to the divisions between that tradition and both Eastern Orthodoxy and Protestantism. He is pivotal in the Western Church's becoming *Roman* Catholic. He was a very influential pope at a crucial turning point in

---

[6]Augustine *On Grace and Free Will* 28, in NPNF 5:455.
[7]Augustine *On Nature and Grace* 2, in NPNF 5:122.

the Western Church's history as well as a major interpreter of Augustine's theology and promoter of monastic piety and life-style. He is often considered by church historians the last church father as well as the first medieval pope and theologian in the West.

During his tenure as bishop of Rome, Pope Gregory I provided a rule (set of guidelines) for all Western bishops that is summarized in his major existing work, *The Book of Pastoral Rule.* He also launched a great missionary effort to convert the pagan peoples of Britain and the Arian barbarian tribes of Europe to Catholic Christianity. He built up monastic communities and gave them charters to control vast territories of Europe for the purpose of establishing firm Christian footholds throughout it. Crucial to our story, Gregory created a hybrid of Augustine's monergistic view of salvation and a semi-Pelagian synergism that has deeply influenced Roman Catholic theology ever after.

On the one hand, Gregory strongly favored Augustine as the greatest church father of all. On the other hand, he read and interpreted Augustine through semi-Pelagian lenses. In other words, Gregory's interpretation and application of Augustine's theology is thoroughly synergistic. When Gregory wished to emphasize the sovereignty of God and his grace and denigrate the self-assertion of sinful human beings, he could sound very much like Augustine. When he wanted to warn Christians against taking grace for granted and urge them to greater efforts of self-sacrificing piety (what modern Christians call discipleship), Gregory could sound very much like Pelagius. His own advice to bishops in *The Book of Pastoral Rule* was that preaching involves two tasks: comforting the afflicted and afflicting the comfortable.

Gregory expresses the Augustinian-Pelagian tension most paradoxically in his soteriology. Once, after emphasizing grace to the point where he *almost* affirmed monergism with

Augustine, Gregory wrote, "Even the predestination itself to the eternal kingdom is so arranged by the omnipotent God that the elect attain it from their own effort."[8] For Gregory, "prayers, penance, masses, intercession, works—all are forms of human effort mediating with the divine."[9] No one would be capable of performing these efforts in any redemptive way apart from assisting grace. But when a person's will and effort cooperate with that grace, so that the person perseveres to the end and goes to the eternal kingdom, this person may be said to have been "predestined to salvation." Electing grace must be activated. In Gregory's mind there was nothing automatic about it.

What is it, then, that a person must do to activate grace so that he or she becomes one of God's elect? According to Gregory, one must be crucified with Christ in order to benefit from Christ's cross and its grace: "Indeed . . . Christ did not fulfill everything for us. To be sure, he redeemed everyone through the Cross, but it is left that he who strives to be redeemed and reign with him should be crucified with him."[10] According to Gregory, being crucified with Christ means extreme repentance, including penitential acts of self-sacrifice, a general rational self-denial of bodily pleasures that hinder spirituality, active participation in the sacramental life of the church, and works of love, such as giving to the poor. The person who truly wishes to please God, become assured of divine election and escape from the pangs of purgatory ought to live the life of a monk, which is the life of the "perfect penitent." For Gregory physical pleasure itself is an enticement to sin, if not actual sin. Sexual intercourse even within marriage is a sin except for the purpose of procreation, and even then, if the act involves any lust or bodily pleasure, it

---

[8]Gregory, quoted in Carole Straw, *Gregory the Great: Perfection in Imperfection* (Berkeley: University of California Press, 1988), p. 140.
[9]Ibid.
[10]Ibid., p. 159.

may involve guilt.[11] If a person wishes to be a "perfect penitent" and be "secure of pardon" and assured of heaven, he or she will surely join a monastic order and deny the body all kinds of pleasures that may be technically allowed by God but contain within themselves the seeds of temptation.

A GREAT RIFT DIVIDES THE TALE IN TWO

The Western Church that became Roman Catholic has always also considered itself orthodox. The Eastern Church that became what we today call Eastern Orthodox has always considered itself catholic. It is merely by convention that people have come to call one "Catholic" and the other "Orthodox." By no means do members of the Church of Rome concede that the Eastern Church is more orthodox than it is. Nor do members of the Eastern Orthodox Church consider the Church of Rome more catholic than it is.

We have seen some of the factors that contributed to the drift of the Western Church away from the Eastern Church, so that by the early Middle Ages it often acted on its own, as if the Eastern Church did not exist. That split was not formal or official, however. If asked, the bishops of the Western Church would have acknowledged the Eastern bishops as genuine Christians, even if a bit odd in their beliefs and practices. The same would have been true of the Eastern bishops if asked about the Western ones.

Just as there were certain pivotal figures and controversies that helped create what we now call Roman Catholicism, so the Eastern Church experienced its own controversies and had its own uniquely Byzantine thinkers who shaped it into the Eastern Orthodox tradition and family of churches. These differences between the East and West eventually came to a head in

---

[11]Gregory *The Book of Pastoral Rule of Saint Gregory the Great* 27, in NPNF2 12:56-58.

two controversies that precipitated a permanent schism in the Christian church.

The first controversy involved the office of the pope. Eastern Christians of the ninth and tenth centuries looked to the West and saw the bishop of Rome attempting to dominate all the rest illegitimately, setting himself up as "pope," or father over all other bishops. They accused the Latins of attempting to force a "monarchy of the pope" on all Christendom and resisted the bishop of Rome's attempts to dominate the East. The Eastern Church considered every orthodox bishop a true successor of Peter, not just the bishop of Rome, and it considered the great sees of Christianity—Rome, Constantinople, Antioch, Alexandria and Jerusalem—equal in dignity, power and authority. The East was willing to acknowledge the patriarch of Rome as "first among equals" but considered that a purely honorary title.

The second controversy, and the one that became the immediate cause of the schism, was over the *filioque* clause in the Latin version of the Nicene Creed. Virtually everyone agrees that the original Greek version of the Niceno-Constantinopolitan Creed of 381 did not contain the phrase "and the Son" *(filioque)* after the portion in which the Holy Spirit is said to proceed "from the Father":

> We believe in the Holy Spirit,
> the Lord, the giver of life,
> who proceeds from the Father *[and the Son]*.
> With the Father and the Son he is worshiped and
>   glorified.
> He has spoken through the Prophets.

The phrase in brackets—"and the Son"—is an English translation of the Latin *filioque* and appears in almost all Western versions of the Nicene Creed. How did it come to be there? That is what no one knows for sure. The Eastern bishops, when they heard about it in Constantinople around 850, insisted that it be taken out for two reasons. First, they loudly protested that the West had no right to alter the basic creed of Christendom without consulting the Eastern Church. Second, they argued that it revealed a deep theological difference between Eastern ideas of the Trinity, which they considered the only truly orthodox ones, and Western ideas of the Trinity rooted in Augustinian thinking, which they considered heterodox (unorthodox verging on heretical).

Leaders of the Western Church would not budge on the issue. Indeed, they condemned as heretical any version of the creed that omitted the *filioque* clause. In response, the Eastern bishops and emperors began hurling accusations of heresy at the pope and bishops of the West. In the end, the two churches declared one another excommunicated from the Great Church. The patriarch of Constantinople in 1054, Michael Cerularius, declared of the bishop of Rome, "The pope is a heretic!"[12] Pope Leo IX's representatives in Constantinople entered the Hagia Sophia cathedral, placed on the high altar a declaration of excommunication against the patriarch and the bishops in fellowship with him, and stalked out. The rift has never been healed.

SCENE CHANGE: SCHOLASTICS REVIVE AND ENTHRONE THEOLOGY

Even as the rift between Eastern and Western Christendom was being made official, Western theology was striking out in a new direction: Scholasticism. The term *Scholasticism* designates a particular approach to Christian theology that gradually came to dominate in the West from about 1100 until its decline dur-

---

[12]Jaroslav Pelikan, *The Christian Tradition: A History of the Development of Doctrine*, vol. 2, *The Spirit of Eastern Christendom, 600-1700* (Chicago: University of Chicago Press, 1974), p. 171.

ing the fourteenth and fifteenth centuries. The Scholastic movement "attempted a methodological and philosophical demonstration of Christian theology as inherently rational and consistent" within the cultural context of medieval Europe.[13] Western Scholastic theology pushed the concern for rationality in theology to new heights.

Anselm and Abelard Speculate About the Incarnation

At the fountainhead of Scholasticism stands Anselm, archbishop of Canterbury (1033-1109). Anselm's claim to fame in the history of Western philosophy is his formulation of the so-called ontological argument for the existence of God, about which many books have been written. It constitutes a marvelous example of Scholastic rationalism as well as of Anselm's genius. To Christian theology he contributed a new model of the atonement (i.e., the meaning of Christ's sacrifice on the cross). Although this theory finds adumbrations earlier in patristic theology, Anselm's version, known as the satisfaction theory of the atonement, represents a quantum leap beyond any doctrine of Christ's reconciling work on behalf of God and humanity before it. Anselm is also known for his staunch opposition to secular or lay control of the church by kings. As archbishop of Canterbury, head of the Catholic Church in England under the pope, Anselm suffered exile twice for refusing to grant the Norman king of England authority over church affairs.

Here we will focus on Anselm's theological contribution: his new model of the atonement. *Atonement* simply means "reconciliation," and in theology the term usually refers to the act of God in Jesus Christ or the act of Jesus Christ as a human being on the cross by which humans are reconciled to God and vice versa. Most Christians in the West during Anselm's age

---

[13]B. B. Price, *Medieval Thought: An Introduction* (Oxford: Blackwell, 1992), p. 120.

thought of Christ's great sacrifice on the cross along the lines
of what is known as the ransom theory. This had been laid out
in its clearest form by Pope Gregory the Great around 600,
although many before him and after him put their own individual touches on it. Gregory used many images to explain the
effect of Christ's death on the cross on humanity, but his favorite was the cross as the "fishhook" on which God placed the
"bait" of Jesus Christ in order to snare the devil and free
humanity from its captivity to him.

Anselm considered this theory of the atonement—which
had become almost universal in the preaching of the Roman
Catholic Church throughout the so-called Dark Ages—an insult
to God. As the Being greater than which none can be conceived,
God does not have to trick the devil, because he is in no way
beholden to him. If the only problem is that humanity has
become captive to Satan and his kingdom, God could simply
invade, conquer the evil forces, and release humankind from
captivity. He would not have to bargain with or trick Satan.

Anselm sought an explanation of the atonement that would
explain why Jesus Christ had to be both truly human and truly
divine and that would be both rational and fully consistent with
Scripture and the church's tradition. Exile from Canterbury in
1098 afforded Anselm the leisure time and opportunity to write
Cur Deus Homo? or *Why God Became Man*. The key question discussed in the book is "Why, and with what necessity, did God
become man, and redeem human beings by his death,
although he could have accomplished this by other means?"[14]
Anselm's alternative to the ransom theory has come to be
called the satisfaction theory because it centers on the medieval concept of a vassal's paying "satisfaction" to a lord when

---

[14]Joseph M. Colleran, "Introduction: St. Anselm's Life," in *Anselm of
Canterbury, Why God Became Man and The Virgin Conception and Original Sin,* trans. Joseph M. Colleran (Albany, N.Y.: Magi, 1969), pp. 34-
35.

he has broken the feudal contract. Anselm found in this cus-
tom the perfect analogy for explaining why God sent his Son in
the form of a human being to die a sinner's death though he
was not at all a sinner. In essence, the theory says that Christ
paid a debt that all humanity owes to God because of disobedience. God's justice demands payment of a satisfaction, or else
the order of the universe would be disrupted. The needed satisfaction is like a debt to God's honor that humanity must
repay, but humanity is incapable of repaying it without suffering complete loss in hell. God in his mercy provides a perfect
substitutionary sacrifice that satisfies his own honor and pre-
serves the moral order of the universe: the price is his own Son.

Not everyone was satisfied with Anselm's new theory of
atonement. One dissenter was the great medieval scholastic
genius Peter Abelard (1079-1142). We know much about
Abelard's personal life because he wrote an autobiography,
The Story of My Misfortunes. Abelard's tormented and tortured
life was even made into a Hollywood feature movie, which
unfortunately tended to focus all too much on the lurid aspects
of his love affair with the lovely Héloïse.

Like Anselm, Abelard disagreed with the traditional ransom
theory, but he also disagreed with Anselm's satisfaction theory.
Instead, he proposed a view that has been called the moral
influence or moral example theory of how Christ's death on
the cross reconciles humanity with God. Abelard's model of the
atonement emphasizes God's love rather than God's honor or
wrath. According to Abelard, what humanity needs is a new
motive for action, not a compensation paid to God on its
behalf. He considered that the satisfaction theory as well as the
ransom theory left humanity out of the process of reconciliation altogether and portrayed the God of the cross as concerned with only his own honor and cosmic justice. Abelard's
mind was captivated by Jesus' parable of the prodigal son
whose father was always waiting for him to return. The effect

of the cross is toward humanity, not toward God. God, according to Abelard, does not need to be reconciled to humanity.
God already loves us. Our problem is that we do not realize this
and because of our sin and ignorance live in alienating fear of
God. The cross of Jesus is an act of God's love that inspires new
motives for our actions: we see how much God loves us, and we
begin to love in return. Unfortunately for Abelard, many of his
views were condemned by a synod of bishops in Paris before
he died. He died while traveling to Rome to appeal his case to
the pope.

Thomas Aquinas at the Height of Scholasticism

One name stands out above all others as the Scholastic thinker
par excellence: Thomas Aquinas (1224/5-1274). It is impossible to overestimate his importance for the story of Christian
theology and especially for the story of Roman Catholic theology. Like Augustine, Aquinas wrote on almost every conceivable topic related to the university curriculum. He was a true
encyclopedist, and therefore it is difficult to touch on even a
few of his ideas and contributions.

One of Aquinas's frequently cited contributions to the story
of theology is commonly called his five "proofs for the existence of God." The "five ways" (quinque viae) are a collection of
Aristotelian and Scholastic demonstrations that rest on the
connections between changeable things and the implied initiator of change, causes and the first cause, contingent and necessary things, gradations of things, and final causes. What has
often been noted about these five ways is that they seem to
prove the existence of God without recourse to faith or revelation; they seem to depend solely on reason. However, as William Placher has observed after a closer inspection of them,
they are not really these kinds of "proofs" at all. This is made
plain by the fact that Aquinas does *not* conclude each argument
with a triumphant "therefore God exists" but rather with a

shrug: "to which everyone gives the name 'God,'" or "and this we call 'God.'"[15] The five ways do not necessarily represent Aquinas's way but rather are collected examples of how others have gone about demonstrating God's existence.

Thomas Aquinas's own way to God can be followed only so far by reason alone. Reason can establish God's existence. Faith is required to know God's character and attributes, and such knowledge is always expressed analogically. Aquinas distinguished three ways to use words. One might use words in a straightforward, univocal fashion. In the sentences "I have a blue shirt" and "Her motorcycle is blue," "blue" is used in exactly the same way. But in the sentence "I feel blue today," "blue" is used to indicate not a color but a feeling—here "blue" is used equivocally (the same word with a different meaning).

When speaking of God, we cannot imagine that our words apply in a direct, one-to-one, univocal correlation between earthly things and divine things. In the sentence "God is wise," "wise" does not mean the same thing as it means in the sentence "Socrates is wise." "Wise" is being used analogously—it means something similar in the two cases but not exactly the same. This is Aquinas's third and preferred way to use language in reference to God. One might say, of course, God's wisdom is like that of humans with the exception that God is infinitely wiser than humans. But such an observation only touches on the superficial level of the analogy. Aquinas suggests that we use analogy not just because God possesses quantitatively more (even infinitely more) wisdom or goodness or justice than we do. In point of fact, God's wisdom is of a different quality and kind from human wisdom.[16] All descriptions of God are nothing more than analogies, according to Aquinas, because we are say-

---

[15]William C. Placher, *The Domestication of Transcendence: How Modern Thinking About God Went Wrong* (Louisville, Ky.: Westminster John Knox, 1996), p. 24.

[16]Ibid., p. 31.

ing what God is *like;* we are not in a position to say, nor do we have the words to say exactly what God *is.* Aquinas recognizes that our words, like our knowledge of God, always fall drastically short of encompassing the reality of God. In fact, our words usually show more of what we do not understand about God than what we do understand. In this life we see in a mirror dimly, then we shall see face to face. Yet Aquinas does not despair because God has revealed himself in Christ. This revelation makes it possible for us to speak truthfully and faithfully about what God is like, just as Jesus spoke truthfully and faithfully about what the kingdom of heaven is like.

Nominalists, Reformers and Humanists Challenge the Medieval Norm

William of Ockham (1280/90-1349), a Franciscan friar, began to test the load-bearing capacity of Aquinas's threefold use of language. To distinguish whether "blue" or "wise" is being used univocally, equivocally, or analogically, one must first have a concept or idea of "blueness" or "wisdom." Indeed, Ockham intuited that the *concept* is primary and Aquinas's three uses of language are just three ways of putting concepts to work. Concepts are the basic building blocks of knowledge. Concepts name and classify things and, of course, should not be substituted for *what* they name (this is the starting point of a philosophical position called conceptualism or nominalism). In other words, concepts are simply how we name things in reality and should not be confused with reality itself. The problem arises when we try to know God conceptually or to name God sufficiently. God cannot be reduced to a concept like "eternal Father" or even the idea of some unchangeable essence like "Being." We do not have direct, experiential access to such divine qualities and therefore can never be certain of them. What we do have access to are the *effects* of God's will: the effects of God's activity in nature and in history, especially as recorded in the Bible. Accordingly, for Ockham, God must be defined primarily in terms of his will. All we can know of God for certain is that he wills to act. God's will must be defined as God's absolute, unconditional power to do whatever God wills to do. This is a fearsome, awesome, and even frightening God.

Not only were theological tensions such as these building in the medieval world, but there was religious unrest. John Wycliffe (1330-1384) was born in William of Ockham's homeland, England, about the time that Ockham died in exile of the plague. One of Wycliffe's claims to fame is his Bible translation work. Of more importance for our story of theology are the convictions that compelled Wycliffe to initiate that work. He believed the pope was corrupt and should be divested of his power to govern the church. The church should be governed by the people of God through their representatives rather than by the hierarchical structure of clergy. If this were to happen, Wycliffe realized, the people would need access to the Bible in a language they could understand and use. His ideas about the church and access to the Bible influenced the great Bohemian reformer John Hus, who was burned at the stake in 1417 but left a legacy that later resulted in Martin Luther's being known as "the Saxon Hus." Thus Wycliffe's theology also indirectly influenced Luther. Further, his followers in England, known as Lollards, helped bring about the Reformation there two hundred years after his death.

These brief snapshots of Wycliffe and Ockham do not begin to reveal the turmoil in which European culture was immersed by the fourteenth and fifteenth centuries. Nationalism was on the rise, the bubonic plague was decimating the population, and the church was falling into ruin. The once great dream of a totally unified Europe led by the pope and emperor working together under God was fading quickly as the church fell under the control of the French kings and the papacy moved to Avignon in France (1309-1377), and as kings of nations that were supposed to be part of the Holy Roman Empire went to war against one another. The nadir of the medieval church and its respect and authority was reached in the Great Schism of the West, when two and then three men managed to lay claim to the office of pope simultaneously (1378-1417). To complicate things, a new cultural mood of freedom, education and artistry was sweeping the elite societies of Europe—the Renaissance.

The mood of the Renaissance can be summed up in one word: *humanism,* a rediscovery and new appreciation of human capacity, intellect, arts, and literature. The humanism of the Renaissance, however, was not "secular." Rather, it was a belief in the cultural creativity of the human person, rejecting the Augustinian pessimism about humanity that had reigned supreme for a thousand years. One of the greatest humanists of this era was in no sense a secularist but rather a highly intellectual monk, Erasmus of Rotterdam (1466-1535). Erasmus is perhaps best remembered for his production of a critical edition of the Greek New Testament in 1514. His humanist commitments are most clearly revealed in his debates with Martin Luther over the issue of free will. Erasmus rejected any theology that belittled, overrode, or neglected the free will and responsibility of all humans. He held to a robust understanding of human nature and potential.

It was evident to everyone living around the turn of the sixteenth century that the world was changing, shedding the medieval habit and donning a new era. Christianity had to change too. Christian theology desperately needed revising, reforming, and in some cases, rewriting.

Act IV

Reforming, Revising and Rewriting the Story

At the dawn of the sixteenth century, Christian theology in Europe was in trouble. The popular theology of the church had fallen prey to ritualism, superstitions, and lifeless Scholasticism. Some church leaders and theologians of Roman Catholicism were implying that grace was a commodity to be earned or even bought. *Merit* had become a key term in Catholic soteriology (doctrine of salvation). One could be truly saved only to the extent that he or she had gained sufficient merit before God through faith and works of love. *Faith* had come to be interpreted as faithfulness to the teachings and practices of the official church, and *works of love* had come to be interpreted as buying indulgences, paying for masses for souls in purgatory and taking expensive pilgrimages to view relics, as well as giving alms to the poor, doing penance, participating in the sacraments, and carrying out devotional practices such as prayer and meditation. By implication, salvation became available only to those who met certain standards of meritorious actions. The "protest" that

constitutes Protestantism takes issue with this claim. Those who
protested the reigning Catholic view of salvation had to ask
themselves: *How, then, is one saved?*

THE PROTESTANT REFORMATION
Martin Luther's Justification by Grace Through Faith

Most historians date the dawn of the great sixteenth-century
Reformation of church and theology to a single day in 1517.
On October 31 of that year, an Augustinian monk and professor of theology at the University of Wittenberg named Martin
Luther (1483-1546) nailed ninety-five theses (points for debate)
to the cathedral church door in the city where he taught. His
theses implied that the official church of Western Christendom—the Church of Rome—was in serious error. Within
months, all of Europe was reading Luther's theses due to the
new invention of Johannes Gutenberg: the movable-type print-
ing press. Pope Leo X read them and declared that the Saxon
monk must have been drunk.

From 1518 until 1520 Luther engaged in debates with leading
Roman Catholic scholars who defended the authority of the
pope to sell indulgences and remit the temporal consequences of
sins (e.g., purgatory). He also wrote several reforming treatises on
the church and its theology and appealed to the German princes
to side with him against Rome. The debates were halted when
Luther was excommunicated by the pope in 1520 and called to
appear before the emperor Charles V at his imperial court (Diet)
in the city of Worms in 1521. When ordered by the pope's representative to recant his "heretical" views, Luther declared, "My
conscience is captive to the Word of God. Thus I cannot and will
not recant, for going against my conscience is neither safe nor
salutary. I can do no other, here I stand, God help me. Amen."[1]

---

[1]Heiko Oberman, *Luther: Man Between God and the Devil,* trans. Eileen
Walliser-Scharzbart (New York: Doubleday, 1992), p. 203.

Luther was banned as an outlaw by the emperor but protected by his prince, Frederick "the Wise" of Saxony. Under Frederick's protection, Luther continued his reformation until his death in 1546. Luther's contributions to Western civilization and to Christianity are innumerable. Most significant, perhaps, he laid out the three cries of the Reformation: justification by grace through faith, *sola scriptura* (Scripture alone is the authority for Christian belief and practice), and the doctrine of the priesthood of the believer (by which every believer is given access to God, not needing a priest to mediate between the person and God). Here we will focus on the first theme, justification by grace through faith alone.

Justification is the act by which God declares a person to be in a right relationship with himself, that is, righteous. So to the question "How is one saved?" Luther would have answered, "As Romans 3:21-30 testifies, you are justified before God by God's own grace in Christ through faith alone." Luther considered this the heart of soteriology and considered soteriology the heart of all theology. For him, "the doctrine of justification is not simply one doctrine among others but the basic and chief article of faith with which the church stands or falls, and on which its entire doctrine depends."[2] In order to understand Luther's concept of justification, it is essential to understand the medieval Catholic teaching against which it stood. According to Catholic doctrine—stretching back at least a thousand years to Augustine—justification is the gradual process by which a sinner is made actually righteous internally by having God's own righteousness infused through the grace of baptism, faith, works of love and the entire penitential life. Only when the sinner is so transformed that he or she is no longer really a sinner at all does God justify in the full and complete sense.

---

[2]Paul Althaus, *The Theology of Martin Luther*, trans. Robert C. Shultz (Philadelphia: Fortress, 1966), p. 225.

Baptismal grace that washes away the guilt of original sin must become habitual grace that grows within through sacraments and penance and must eventually become sinless perfection. For traditional Catholicism, justification comes gradually through the salvation process and is completed only at its end.

Luther despaired of ever finding justification this way. He had been baptized and had become the "perfect penitent" by entering a monastery and going to confession in true contrition several times daily. He had even tried whipping and half-starving himself as well as sleeping on the cold stone floor of his monastery cell. Yet his conscience was still troubled, and God's countenance still seemed angry so long as he considered it in light of his own imperfect goodness. He felt that he could never fully please God no matter how hard he tried. His study of Scripture led him to a much deeper sense of human sinfulness than the medieval Catholic system of salvation presupposed. Luther came to believe that "man . . . sins even when he does the best he can, even in his best works."[3] Where then could there be any hope for justification? His alternative doctrine began with his insights that "I am not good and righteous, but Christ is" and that a "sweet and joyful exchange" between Christ's goodness and righteousness and the human person's own sinfulness and unrighteousness took place on the cross and is of full benefit the moment one has faith and believes in it. "As bride and bridegroom exchange possessions in a marriage, so the sinner receives justification from Christ, and Christ takes over the Christian's sins."[4]

This joyful exchange takes place both on the cross through Christ's death and in the Christian's life as soon as he or she believes the Word of God and trusts in Christ alone for salvation. Nothing is necessary for it other than the cross in history,

---

[3]Ibid., p. 149.
[4]Oberman, *Luther,* p. 184.

the gospel proclaimed and faith in the heart of the sinner. No penitential acts can add anything. The merits of Christ imputed to the sinner by God cannot be increased. The righteousness gained is Christ's; it is "alien" to us: "through faith in Christ . . . Christ's righteousness becomes our righteousness and all that he has becomes ours, he himself becomes ours."[5] Luther made clear in the context that this justifying righteousness never becomes a person's own possession. It remains forever completely Christ's. Furthermore, it does not change the person receiving it into an actually righteous person, although it provides a new motive for pleasing God—gratitude. The person receiving Christ's righteousness remains a sinner through and through. Such a person remains in a constant state of *simul justus et peccator*—"simultaneously righteous and a sinner." Because of Christ received by faith, God sees the sinner as righteous while the sinner is still just that—a sinner: "thus a Christian man is both righteous and a sinner, holy and profane, an enemy of God and yet a child of God."[6]

At the same time Luther was beginning his reform of church and theology in Germany, another Reformer was inaugurating a Protestant revolution in Switzerland. Ulrich Zwingli is considered by the Swiss a national hero, and Swiss Protestants generally believe that his breakthrough to Protestantism was completely independent of Luther. The same cannot be said of his younger French-born Swiss colleague John Calvin of Geneva. He was influenced by Lutheran teachings while a university student in Paris. Together Zwingli and Calvin helped reform Switzerland and establish what is known as the

---

[5]Martin Luther, "Two Kinds of Righteousness in Christ," in *Martin Luther's Basic Theological Writings*, ed. Timothy Lull (Minneapolis: Fortress, 1989), p. 156.

[6]Martin Luther, "A Commentary on St. Paul's Epistle to the Galatians," in *Martin Luther: Selections from His Writings*, ed. John Dillenberger (New York: Anchor, 1962), p. 130.

"Reformed" branch of Protestantism—the major European counterpart to Lutheranism, which spawned the Presbyterian and Puritan movements in Great Britain.

Zwingli and Calvin Organize Protestant Thought

Luther never published a systematic theology, and his thoughts remained largely inchoate if not incoherent. Paradox was his normal mode of expression, because he believed that God and God's Word are ultimately mysterious and beyond human comprehension. The Swiss Reformers were more intent on organizing and systematizing the new Protestant theology. In the process of doing that they added their own spin, so that the theology stemming from their works is usually identified as Reformed, while that stemming from Luther is called Lutheran or Evangelical. (In some parts of Europe *Evangelical* simply means Protestant as opposed to Roman Catholic.)

Ulrich Zwingli (1484-1531), "the people's priest" at Zurich, is most often remembered for his debates with Luther over the Lord's Supper (which he interpreted as a memorial meal in remembrance and celebration of Christ's sacrifice but which Luther interpreted as the real presence of Christ to believers). However, Zwingli is better memorialized as the initiator of reform in Switzerland and as the father of Reformed Protestantism.

Zwingli's distinctive contribution to theology comes from his understanding of God's providence. While Luther believed and taught that God is the all-determining reality, Zwingli placed the sovereignty of God in a special position within Christian theology. Luther treated God's sovereignty as a part of the gospel of grace, but Zwingli, and later Calvin, treated God's sovereignty as a first principle of Christian thought. That is not to say it appears first in his system of theology. Rather, it has a certain pride of place among all the doctrines as Reformed theology's central organizing theme, the hub that holds everything together. For Luther, that would be the doctrine of salvation (justification) by grace through faith alone. For Zwingli, Calvin and their Reformed colleagues, it became the doctrine of God's all-determining sovereignty and power.

On the basis of reason and Scripture, Zwingli arrived at the strongest conceivable doctrine of God's meticulous providential and sovereign rule over everything. If God is God, he argued, then absolutely nothing else can have any independent power or determination. Zwingli wrote in *On Providence,* "I defined Providence as the rule over and direction of all things in the universe. For if anything were guided by its own power or insight, just so far would the wisdom and power of our Deity be deficient."[7] God's providential rule is eternal and unchangeable, the cause of everything that happens, including both good and evil, and rules out anything contingent, fortuitous or accidental. God and God alone is the "sole cause" over everything, and all other so-called causes are merely "instruments of the divine working."[8]

John Calvin (1509-1564) organized and extended these teachings on providence, as well as Zwingli's teachings on infant baptism, predestination, and Scripture. John Calvin was born near Noyon, France, on July 10, 1509; he died in Geneva, Switzerland, on May 27, 1564. In Geneva, an independent republic that later became part of Switzerland, Calvin virtually ruled as "chief pastor"; the French Protestant Reformer established the Genevan Academy, to which Protestants flocked from all over Europe. Throughout the times of Protestant persecutions in Scotland and England, the seminary in Geneva attracted future Reformers such as John Knox (1514-1572), who succeeded in turning Scotland into a nation modeled after the

---

[7]Ulrich Zwingli, "On the Providence of God," in *On Providence and Other Essays,* ed. Samuel Jackson and William John Hinke (Durham, N.C.: Labrynth, 1983), p. 137.
[8]Ibid., p. 157.

Swiss city. It was Knox who proclaimed Geneva and its academy under Calvin and his successor, Theodore Beza, "the most perfect school of Christ since the days of the apostles."

With regards to his theology of God and providence, Calvin, like Luther and Zwingli, viewed God as the all-determining reality and taught God's meticulous providence over nature and history. Sometimes Calvin referred certain events in history to God's "permission," but overall he saw God as the ultimate cause of everything and taught that absolutely nothing happens or can happen apart from God's determination "by his decree." Like Zwingli, Calvin denied contingency; nothing happens by accident. Nor does God merely foresee or foreknow what is going to happen in the future. Rather, "God by the bridle of his providence turns every event whatever way he wills,"[9] and "what for us seems a contingency, faith recognizes to have been a secret impulse from God."[10] Does this mean that even the fall of Adam and Eve was foreordained by God? Certainly Adam and Eve were guilty of going against God's will, just as we are when we disobey God's law. Even so, Calvin affirmed, "The first man fell because the Lord had judged it to be expedient; why he so judged is hidden from us. Yet it is certain that he so judged because he saw that thereby the glory of his name is duly revealed."[11] For Calvin, everything that happens redounds to God's glory, even if we humans cannot see how, and God's glory is the purpose why everything happens, even if we are unable to reconcile it with love, mercy or justice.

Even though belief in double predestination is often simply called Calvinism and many people have thought it to be the central organizing principle of Calvin's theology and his

---

[9]John Calvin, *Institutes of the Christian Religion*, trans. Ford Lewis Battles (Philadelphia: Westminster Press, 1960), vol. 1, 1.16.9, p. 209.
[10]Ibid., p. 210.
[11]Ibid., vol. 2, 3.23.8, p. 957.

greatest contribution, "on closer examination, one is impressed with the unoriginality of Calvin's doctrine of election. His teaching on this subject is in all essentials identical to what we have already observed in Luther and Zwingli."[12] Calvin affirmed that in both Scripture and Christian tradition "God is said to have ordained from eternity those whom he wills to embrace in love, and those upon whom he wills to vent his wrath."[13] He acknowledged an apparent conflict between this doctrine and 1 Timothy 2:3-4 and 2 Peter 3:9, both of which suggest a universal will of God for salvation. Calvin's solution was to posit a dual will of God—one revealed and one secret. God's revealed will offers mercy and pardon to all who repent and believe. God's secret will foreordains some to eternal damnation and renders it certain that they will sin and never repent (Rom 9:10-23). Impatient with those who objected to this doctrine of two wills and double predestination as unjust, Calvin declared, "For as Augustine truly contends, they who measure divine justice by the standard of human justice are acting perversely."[14]

Radical Reformers Recover the Roots of Christianity

The entire collection of Protestant Reformers and their followers in the sixteenth century may be divided into two major categories: the Magisterial Reformers and the Radical Reformers. *Radical* simply means "going back to the roots," and of course, all of the Protestants intended to recover the true New Testament gospel from the layers of medieval tradition that they saw surrounding and burying it. Yet certain Protestant Reformers were more radical than the rest, and they have come to be lumped together as "the Radical

---

[12]Timothy George, *Theology of the Reformers* (Nashville: Broadman, 1988), p. 232.

[13]Calvin *Institutes*, vol. 2, 3.24.17, p. 985.

[14]Ibid, p. 987.

Reformers" or simply "radical Protestants" because of their common characteristics.[15]

The main magisterial Reformers included such figures as Luther, Zwingli and Calvin. Their associates and followers in various European cities and countries constituted the magisterial Reformation because they all intended to establish one true Christian church and commonwealth in their country with the support of *magistrates*—a general term for secular authorities such as princes, judges and city council members. The magisterial Reformers envisioned some form of cooperation between church and state and sought to drive out of their territories all Romanists (Roman Catholics) and heretics. For the most part these magisterial Protestants, whether Lutheran, Reformed or Anglican, recognized a relative authority in the earliest creeds of Christendom, insisted on infant baptism, allowed only one legal form of Christianity in their territories and advocated the power of the secular authorities to wage war and persecute religious nonconformists.

The Radical Reformation includes all those Protestants of sixteenth-century Europe who believed in the principle of separation of church and state, renounced coercion in matters of religious belief, emphasized the experience of regeneration (being "born again") by the Spirit of God over forensic justification, and rejected infant baptism in favor of believer's baptism or Spirit baptism, a distinctive for which they were labeled "Anabaptists"—that is, *re*baptizers. Some noteworthy names in this camp are Balthasar Hubmaier, Menno Simons, Felix Manz and Conrad Grebel. They eschewed Christian magistrates and often sought to live apart from the rest of society as much as possible. Some founded Christian communes. Most embraced

---

[15]This delineation of the two types of sixteenth-century Protestant Reformers is drawn loosely from George H. Williams, *The Radical Reformation* (Philadelphia: Westminster Press, 1962), pp. xxiii-xxxi.

Christian pacifism and simple lifestyles. Some rejected formal theological training and professional clergy. All emphasized practical Christian living more than creeds and confessions of doctrinal belief.

The radical Protestants were "the Protestants of Protestantism." They protested what they saw as the halfway measures taken by Luther and the other magisterial Reformers in purifying the church of Roman Catholic elements. The radical Reformers were trying to restore the first-century, apostolic shape to Christianity. Only when the church was made to look and act like the original New Testament church would the Protestant Reformation would be complete.

THE ENGLISH REFORMATION

The English Reformation began very differently from the other Protestant Reformations in Europe. King Henry VIII (1491-1547) wanted to divorce his wife and marry another because his wife, Catherine of Aragon, had not produced a male heir to the throne. For political as much as religious reasons (Catherine was an aunt of Charles V, emperor of the Holy Roman Empire), the pope could not grant Henry the divorce. So Henry severed the official relationship between the Church of England and Rome. To the post of primate of England he appointed a sympathetic English theologian, Thomas Cranmer (1489-1556), who would legitimize his divorce and remarriage. Cranmer proceeded cautiously to reform England, as much as Henry would allow, along Lutheran lines. Henry was distinctly unsympathetic to the Protestant cause in spite of his gratitude to Cranmer. In 1534 the king declared himself "Supreme Head" of the English Catholic Church, with the archbishop of Canterbury as his subordinate, and burned at the stake both Roman Catholics and Protestants who would not recognize his supremacy. Under Henry the theology of the Church of England remained solidly Catholic but independent of Rome and the pope. His daughter, Elizabeth I, would complete the English Reformation in a similarly mediating way. This "middle-way" Reformation style gave birth to the Church of England, or Anglican Church.

THE ROMAN CATHOLIC COUNTER-REFORMATION

In the 1520s and 1530s various Roman Catholic leaders and theologians called for a new ecumenical council to respond to the sweeping Protestant revolution and perhaps to reform the church from within. On November 11, 1544, Pope Paul III issued a decree calling the nineteenth ecumenical council of the church to meet at the Italian city of Trent beginning in March of the next year. The council would last twenty years. The emperor hoped that the council would bring about reconciliation between Protestants and Roman Catholics and reunite Christendom. He insisted that Lutheran representatives be invited. Unfortunately, the pope had different ideas. He wanted the council to spell out the differences between Protestants and the church of Rome and make clear that the former were heretics and the latter represented the one true church.

With regard to the three cries of the Reformation—justification by grace through faith, *sola scriptura,* and the priesthood of the believer—the Council of Trent decreed the following. Justification was to be understood as "a passing from the state in which man is born of the first Adam, to the state of grace and adoption as sons of God . . . through the second Adam, Jesus Christ our Savior. After the promulgation of the gospel this passing cannot take place without the water of regeneration [baptism] or the desire for it."[16] Furthermore, the council decreed that "justification is not only the remis-

---

[16]John F. Clarkson et al., trans., *The Church Teaches: Documents of the Church in English Translation* (St. Louis, Mo.: Herder, 1961), pp. 231-32.

sion of sins, but sanctification and renovation of the interior man through the voluntary reception of grace and gifts, whereby a man becomes just instead of unjust and a friend instead of an enemy, that he may be an heir in the hope of life everlasting."[17] Thus Trent identified justification with sanctification, treating them as two sides of the same coin of salvation.

The representatives at Trent rejected outright the Protestant notion of Scripture alone. Christian doctrine has two sources of authority: Scripture and tradition. Not only did Trent affirm the authority of extrabiblical traditions, it also anathematized, or condemned, any person who knowingly and willfully rejects or insults them. Furthermore, the council identified the Latin Vulgate as the authentic edition of the Bible (including the so-called apocryphal books) and authorized the Mother Church (Rome) as the final judge of Scripture's meaning. In like fashion, the doctrine of the priesthood of believers was dismissed out of hand. After Trent, any chance of reconciliation between Protestants and Catholics was lost.

WHAT HAPPENS NEXT: PROTESTANTS BEGIN WRITING THEIR OWN STORIES

Some Protestants have the naive impression that nothing of major historical importance happened between the Reformation and the twentieth century; the Reformers restored true Christianity, and it has been that way ever since. This, of course, is not the case. At least five major Protestant movements appeared on the heels of the Reformation, attempting to correct or complete the Reformation in some way. In so doing, Arminians, Pietists, Puritans, Methodists and Deists began to write their own stories.

---

[17]Ibid., p. 233.

Arminius Attempts to Reform Reformed Theology

Throughout the second half of the sixteenth century, the Reformed Protestant theology gradually developed a system of Calvinist doctrine that later came to be summarized with the acronym TULIP. These five points of Calvinism were pronounced and made official doctrine at the Synod of Dort in 1618-1619. Here are the five points in a nutshell:

- Total depravity: humans are dead in trespasses and sins before God sovereignly regenerates them and gives them the gift of salvation. (This usually implies a denial of free will.)

- Unconditional election: God chooses some humans to save before and apart from anything they do on their own. (This leaves open the question whether God actively predestines some to damnation or merely leaves them to their deserved damnation.)

- Limited atonement: Christ died to save only the elect. To say that Christ died for nonelected people implies that his death was ineffective for them. This cannot be the case since Christ's atoning death is always effective. Therefore, atonement must be limited to the elect, leaving the nonelect in the mystery of God's providence.

- Irresistible grace: God's grace cannot be resisted. The elect will receive it and be saved by it. The damned never receive it.

- Perseverance of the saints: The elect will inevitably persevere unto final salvation (eternal security or "once saved, always saved").

Not all Reformed Protestants agreed with these five points. Some, like Jacob Arminius (1560-1609), who had studied in Geneva under Calvin's chief disciple, Theodore Beza, felt that the points summarized by TULIP were a gross, reductionistic distortion of the doctrine of election. Arminius entered a firestorm of controversy when he began to question the rigid understanding of election and predestination of some Reformed theologians.

Arminius did not deny the doctrine of election, but he insisted that it be understood as divine *foreknowledge* of what individuals would freely do with the liberty given them. God knows in advance who will believe and who will not believe. As Paul says in Romans 8:29, "Those whom he foreknew he also predestined to be conformed to the image of his Son, in order that he might be the firstborn within a large family" (NRSV). The doctrine of election, understood as foreknowledge, becomes in essence a doctrine of assurance of salvation. Any and all who, in faith, accept Christ's salvation can rest assured that they will in fact be saved; all who believe can be confident that they have been elected by God to become children of God.

With regard to "limited atonement," Arminius asserts that the saving effects of Christ's death and resurrection are limited to the elect in the following sense: salvation extends only to those who freely choose to believe. The "limited" (if one wants to use that term) effect of Christ's death does not imply that he died for some and not others; Christ died to atone for the sins of all humanity. But salvation is limited to those who believe and does not include those who reject Christ. To be damned is to reject Christ's salvation.

What about "irresistible grace"? Whereas classical Calvinists argued that saving grace is always irresistible, Arminius believed that grace is resistible and that many even in Scripture resisted the grace of God. But how can salvation be "all of grace" if humans are free to either accept or reject it? Arminius answered this question with "prevenient grace," grace that goes before salvation. God is always courting his creation, extending grace and love to everyone in various ways. So long as one does not resist this prevenient grace but allows it to work, it becomes justifying grace. That change is "conversion" and is not a good work but simple acceptance. The human will liberated by pre-

venient grace (an operation of the Holy Spirit within a person)
must cooperate by accepting the need of salvation and allowing
God to give the gift of faith. God will not impose it. Neither can
the sinner earn it. It can only be freely accepted, but even the
ability to accept it is made possible by grace.

Unfortunately, Arminius was never able to defend fully his
interpretation of Calvinism. He died of tuberculosis in the
midst of a public inquisition into his theology by religious and
political leaders. His followers valiantly continued his cause,
but the debate was, for all practical purposes, ended with the
Synod of Dort and the ratification of the five points of TULIP.

Pietists Seek to Renew Lutheran Theology

Just as Arminianism was a reaction to and rejection of post-
Calvin Reformed theology, so Pietism was a reaction to and
rejection of post-Luther Lutheran orthodoxy. The Pietist movement was not interested in introducing new doctrines or even
in radically altering the beliefs of German Lutheranism. Yet it
was more than a movement for spiritual renewal. Its unique
emphases amounted to a shift in theology, even though that
shift was for the most part unconscious and unintended. The
shift may be summed up by saying that before Pietism, Protestant theology focused by and large on the objective nature of
salvation—what God has done *for* people—whereas Pietist theology focused more on the subjective nature of salvation, what
God does *within* people.

Lutheran theology had emphasized the objective nature of
God's work of redemption and had largely eschewed interest in
spiritual experiences of a subjective nature. Believers were
encouraged to accept and affirm God's word of promise given
in Jesus Christ through Scripture and the water of baptism,
quite apart from any emotions they might experience. When a
person came to a minister of the Lutheran state church and
confessed feelings of guilt, condemnation and lack of assur-

ance of salvation, the minister would likely ask, "Have you been baptized?" If the answer was affirmative, the church member would be encouraged to renew the faith of baptism and trust God's promise of forgiveness through its water and the accompanying Word. Baptism was the "landmark" of the believer's relationship with God. Pietists, on the other hand, would ask such a person, "Have you been converted?" and "How is your devotional life?" For them, the "landmark" of true Christianity became personal conversion rather than water baptism, and assurance rested in conversional piety rather than in daily renewal of baptismal faith.

Puritans and Methodists Struggle to Revive English Theology
In a similar fashion to the Arminians and the Pietiests, in England some were dissatisfied with the form of Protestantism that had become dominant. They looked to Geneva and Scotland as models and argued that English church must be "purified" so as to complete the Reformation. These Puritans were thoroughly and persistently Calvinistic. They proclaimed the absolute sovereignty of God and total depravity of humanity. They would have agreed heartily with the five theological points of the Synod of Dort (TULIP), and they condemned Arminianism as a "gangrenous" disease on Christian theology. The only thing a Puritan theologian loved as much as examining and extolling the mysterious ways of providence in history was exploring and proclaiming the stages and aspects of Christian experience in the believing individual. Beyond Calvinism, Puritan theology was characterized by three theological ideas that together compose the Puritan consensus: a purified church, a covenant relationship between God and the elect, and a Christianized society. Each idea had been at least foreshadowed in earlier Protestant theologies, but the Puritans emphasized each one in a unique way and combined them in a distinctly Puritan recipe found nowhere else in the story of Christian theology.

The thinker who made the most convincing and rigorous case for Puritan theology was the American Jonathan Edwards (1703-1757).

Another renewal and reform movement arose within the Church of England just as Puritanism was losing steam. The so-called Great Awakening in England and its North American colonies in the 1740s helped bring about Puritanism's demise and Methodism's birth. Methodism began as a pietist and revivalist movement to breathe new life into the increasingly cold, formal and rationalistic Anglican tradition. John Wesley (1703-1791) and his friend George Whitefield (1714-1770) had no intention of leading a schism or starting a new denomination; they simply wanted to reawaken the hearts of the faithful and offer "methods" of embodying discipleship. Eventually, strained relations between their Methodist societies and the mother church forced John Wesley to allow his lieutenants to split from the Church of England. The Methodist Episcopal Church was born in the United States in 1784, less than a decade before John Wesley's death in 1791. In England the movement became officially independent of the Church of England as a "dissenting church" in 1787. Wesley himself maintained the illusion that his movement would transform the Church of England until he was nearly on his deathbed. Only then did he reluctantly admit that he had founded a new Protestant denomination.

Wesley's special contribution to the story of Protestant theology lies in his distinctive interpretations of two of its classical principles. First, while affirming *sola scriptura*, he developed a view of authority for Christian faith and practice that became known as the Wesleyan quadrilateral. Wesley held to the supreme authority of Scripture over every other source and norm for Christian preaching and living. On the other hand, he included reason, tradition and experience as essential interpretive tools for doing theology. This is the Wesleyan quadrilateral: four essential sources and tools of theology—Scripture, reason, tradition and experience. Second, while affirming *sola gratia et fides,* he emphasized the real possibility of Christian perfection through entire sanctification. Christians should strive for "perfection in love" precisely because it is possible to make progress in that area. The Christian is called to be sanctified in the here and now. These two amendments to classical Protestant theology were controversial in Wesley's own lifetime. They have deeply influenced Methodism and through it much of Protestant Christianity, and continue to be matters of debate within Christianity.

Deists Edit the Storyline to Fit a New Audience

At the same time that Edwards and Wesley were creating modern evangelical Christianity, other religious reformers were trying to move Protestantism in a totally new and different direction led by the head rather than the heart. Deism, or natural religion, a movement of the seventeenth and early eighteenth centuries, tried to reform Protestant theology to make it reasonable and compatible with the budding modern world.

Early Deistic thinkers like John Locke (1632-1704), Matthew Tindal (1657-1733) and John Toland (1670-1722) aimed at developing and defending three main ideas. First, they sought to demonstrate that authentic Christianity is completely consistent with reason. If a belief or moral rule cannot be shown to be consistent with universal standards of rationality, it should not be believed or followed. Although this rule appears uncontroversial, one does not have to look far before one finds key Christian beliefs that might conflict with modern rationality. For instance, Deists considered the doctrine of the Trinity incompatible with natural religion, and although they did not attack it outright, they virtually ignored it. The same is true of almost every other distinctively Christian doctrine.

A second idea common to Deism is that true religion, including true Christianity, is primarily about social and individual morality. Deists tended to reduce religion to a set of basic beliefs about God, immortality of the soul, and rewards and punishments for behavior that were universally accessible to reason and primarily of value only as supports for virtue in this life. Deists were not much interested in metaphysical or theological speculation. If beliefs could not be shown to have some practical value for humanity's progress toward reformation of life, they tended to be actively uninterested in them. They were all convinced, however, that some kind of belief in God and immortality of souls as well as judgment after death was necessary for the progressive reformation of life. Religious beliefs, then, became merely utilitarian supports for ethics in most Deists' minds.

The third and final common notion of Deism is that intelligent, enlightened people ought to be skeptical of all claims of supernatural revelations and miracles. While the eighteenth-century Deists such as Toland and Tindal did not deny these, they clearly relegated them to a lesser status than universal truths of reason and reduced the supernatural element in religion almost to a vanishing point. Later, more radical Deists rejected miracles altogether and opted for a purely naturalistic, demythologized Christianity stripped of everything miraculous. The worldview of Deism was largely shaped by Newtonian physics and its universe ruled by rigid natural laws. It was a "world machine" with little room for divine intervention. Even where Deists acknowledged the miraculous, it these remained a foreign element in their system of thought waiting to be eradicated.

Act V

An Unresolved Plot

At first glance, the Deists discussed at the conclusion of the last chapter seemed to have veered sharply from orthodox, historic Christianity. But with closer inspection, we can see that they were earnestly trying to respond to the burgeoning challenges of a modern world. Up until the dawn of the nineteenth century, traditional church leaders and theologians seem to have been avoiding the modern shift. But eventually no one could escape the recognition that the landscapes of politics, science and philosophy were changing before their eyes.

LIBERAL THEOLOGY ACCOMMODATES TO MODERN CULTURE
Friedrich Schleiermacher (1768-1834) recognized that Christianity must keep pace with the changes or be left in the proverbial dust of time. He was the first professional Protestant theologian to call for sweeping changes in Protestant orthodoxy to encounter and come to terms with the *Zeitgeist* of modernity. Schleiermacher fathered what has come to be called liberal Protestant theology.

Schleiermacher, who was formed as much by his Pietist fam-

ily background as by his Enlightened, modern education,
became a minister of the Reformed Church and served as a
chaplain at a hospital in Berlin and then as professor of theology and university preacher at the University of Halle. In 1806,
when Halle was closed by Napoleon, he moved back to Berlin.
There he pastored the large and influential Trinity Church
and helped found the University of Berlin. He became the
dean of its faculty of theology and gained a reputation throughout Germany as a national hero, powerful preacher and great
intellectual. When he died in 1834, the people of Berlin lined
the streets in mourning as the funeral procession passed.

The liberal flavor of Schleiermacher's Protestantism comes
from his distinctive claim that the essence of religion lies not
in rational proofs of the existence of God, supernaturally
revealed dogmas or churchly rituals and formalities but in a
"fundamental, distinct, and integrative element of human life
and culture"—the feeling *(Gefühl)* of being utterly dependent
on something infinite that manifests itself in and through
finite things.[1]

Schleiermacher removed authoritative, objective revelation
from the center of religion and replaced it with *Gefühl*. The
closest English translation of this term would be "deep inner
awareness." It is often translated "feeling," but that conveys a
wrong impression. For Schleiermacher, both religion in general and Christianity as a positive religion are mainly about a
universal human faculty and experience that he called *Gefühl*.
It is the distinctly human awareness of something infinite
beyond the self on which the self is dependent for everything.

By the time he wrote *The Christian Faith* in 1821, Schleiermacher had come to refer to *Gefühl* as "God-consciousness," and

---

[1]Terrence N. Tice, introduction to Friedrich Schleiermacher, *On Religion: Addresses in Response to Its Cultural Critics,* trans. Terrence N. Tice
(Richmond, Va.: John Knox, 1969), p. 12.

he argued that there is both a universal God-consciousness in humanity and specific religious forms of it in the positive religions. According to Schleiermacher, Christian theology is not so much reflection on supernatural divine revelation as it is the attempt to set forth the Christian religious affections in speech.[2] The key Christian religious affection is the feeling of being totally dependent on the redemptive work of Jesus Christ for one's relationship with God. This is the "essence of Christianity"—a deep awareness of being dependent on God (God-consciousness) and on Jesus Christ as one's link to God. This *Gefühl* formed the authoritative source and norm for Schleiermacher's theology, and even Scripture itself would be not only interpreted but judged by it. Although this principle might strike some as anthropocentric, Schleiermacher was not perturbed. He argued that talk about God is always talk about *human experience of* God. Finite human beings cannot have direct access to God-in-himself; knowledge of God is always mediated by human experience of God, with the Bible being the most significant record of that experience.

The implications of this approach to theology, and hence the liberal nature of this theology, are demonstrated most clearly in Schleiermacher's Christology, or doctrine of Christ. He rejected the traditional doctrine of the two natures of Jesus Christ and replaced it with a Christology based entirely on Jesus' experience of God-consciousness. Jesus Christ, he taught, is completely like the rest of humanity in nature. The only difference is that, unlike other humans, "from the outset he has an absolutely potent God-consciousness."[3] From his birth on, he lived in full awareness of his dependence on God and never sinfully violated that relationship of dependence by

---

[2]Friedrich Schleiermacher, *The Christian Faith,* ed. H. R. Mackintosh and J. S. Stewart, 2nd ed. (Philadelphia: Fortress, 1928), p. 76.
[3]Ibid., p. 367.

asserting his autonomy over against God, his heavenly Father. Schleiermacher expressed his functional Christology (as opposed to an ontological Christology) when he wrote, "The Redeemer, then, is like all men in virtue of the identity of human nature, but distinguished from them all by the constant potency of His God-consciousness, which was a veritable existence of God in Him."[4] According to Schleiermacher, because of this potency of God-consciousness, Jesus Christ was the Savior of humanity because he was able to communicate it in some measure to others through the community he founded known as the church. Schleiermacher denied both the satisfaction and substitution theories of the atonement in favor of something closer to Abelard's moral influence model. Through his life and death, he averred, Jesus Christ draws believers into the power of his own God-consciousness and imparts it to them in some measure. Clearly, Schleiermacher's Christology treats Jesus more as an exalted human being than as God incarnate. It can be justly accused of being more adoptionistic than incarnational.

In the end, metaphysical doctrines such as Christ's divinity, the atonement, and the Trinity could not find a home in Protestant liberalism. They could not be verified by the dictates of reason, nor were they directly accessible to experience (one might have an inner awareness of God, but it seemed unreasonable that one might have a natural awareness of the Trinity). The focus of Christian theology, under the guidance of reason and experience, shifted from doctrine to ethics. This is what has been called the moralization of dogma. Under the influence of the Enlightenment thinker Immanuel Kant, liberal Protestant thinkers insisted on reinterpreting all doctrines and dogmas of Christianity in moral terms, and those that could not be so reinterpreted were neglected if not discarded entirely. Muted

---

[4]Ibid., p. 385.

were the great themes of doctrine developed over hundreds of years. Christianity was virtually reduced to a few simple religious statements and a socialist political and economic program. The heyday of this kind of liberal Protestant theology was the early twentieth century, especially in the United States.

Classical liberal Protestant theology swept through the seminaries and mainstream denominations of Europe and North America with such transformative power and influence that many traditional Protestant thinkers and leaders were caught off guard. But a strong reaction to such a radical reforming movement was bound to set in, and it appeared in most intense form under the label "fundamentalism" in the early decades of the twentieth century.

CONSERVATIVE THEOLOGY HARDENS FUNDAMENTAL CATEGORIES

If the essence of liberal Protestant theology was maximal acknowledgment of the claims of modernity within Christian thought, the essence of fundamentalist theology may be described as maximal acknowledgment of the claims of Protestant orthodoxy against modernity and liberal theology. Its core attitude and approach were what has been called "maximal conservatism" in Christian theology. Its passion was to defend the verbal inspiration and absolute infallibility (inerrancy) of the Bible, as well as all traditional doctrines of Protestant orthodox theology perceived as under attack by modern thought and liberal theology.

As a distinct movement of Protestant Christianity, fundamentalism began around 1910. Scholars debate endlessly the exact time and nature of its birth and even the origin of the label "fundamentalism." Nearly all agree, however, that the publication of a series of booklets called *The Fundamentals* beginning in 1910 was a crucial catalyst and a possible source of the movement's name. Inspired by the great revivals of evangelist Dwight Lyman Moody (1837-1899), dismayed and appalled by the growing influence of liberal theology, and energized by the resurgent Protestant orthodoxy of B. B. Warfield (1851-1921) and others, two wealthy Christian businessmen sponsored the publication and free distribution of twelve collections of essays by leading conservative Protestant scholars. *The Fundamentals* were sent free of charge to thousands of pastors, denominational leaders, professors and even YMCA directors all over the United States.

The Fundamentals tapped into a reservoir of conservative Protestant anxiety and helped to galvanize a conservative response to liberal theology and the increasingly popular and influential social gospel. Throughout the following decade, several groups of antiliberal Christians formulated lists of fundamentals of the faith. Often these lists of essential doctrines were conditioned by liberalism in that they placed at the heart of Christian belief doctrines perceived as threatened by liberalism. Even more to the point, some of the lists included beliefs never before considered essential Christian doctrines by any significant group of Christians. An example is belief in the visible return of Christ. Along with biblical inerrancy, the Trinity, the virgin birth of Christ, the fall of humans into sin, Christ's substitutionary atonement, bodily resurrection and ascension, the belief that Christ would return visibly and bodily to rule and reign on earth for one thousand years before the final resurrection and judgment was elevated from an opinion held by some Christians to a "fundamental of the faith" by the World's Christian Fundamentals Association, founded by leading fundamentalist minister W. B. Riley (1861-1947) in 1919. Even some other very conservative Protestants were shocked by this rigid stance. From about 1910 to 1960, the fundamentalist project became increasingly intense and militantly separatistic as fundamentalist leaders disagreed among themselves about the fundamentals of the faith.

Without any doubt, fundamentalism's main appeal has been at the level of grassroots Christianity. Today literally thousands of pastors and congregations and hundreds of national ministries of various kinds are fundamentalist to some degree. Almost every U.S. city of any size has large, active fundamentalist congregations, flourishing fundamentalist bookstores and often relatively small but established fundamentalist Bible colleges or institutes. More often than not, in the last decades of the twentieth century these churches and institutions dropped the word *fundamentalist* from their names and from their advertising. Many militantly conservative churches and institutions began preferring the label "conservative evangelical" during the 1980s.

NEO-ORTHODOXY TRANSCENDS THE DIVIDE

After the experience of World War I, some Protestants found themselves disenchanted with all the then-current theological alternatives: fundamentalism, liberalism, and traditional Protestant orthodoxy. They were disillusioned with both traditional Protestant orthodoxy and liberal Protestant theology but strongly disagreed with fundamentalism about the Bible. Out of their extreme dissatisfaction, they forged a new theological outlook, now commonly referred to as "neo-orthodoxy." Like every other theological movement discussed here, neo-orthodoxy is notoriously difficult to describe precisely. Not all of its adherents like the label. Many prefer "New Reformation Theology" or "dialectical theology." The movement's founder and prophet, Karl Barth (1886-1968), wished to recover a "theology of the Word of God."[5]

---

[5]Several Barth scholars have argued that Barth should not be placed in the neo-orthodox camp because certain elements of his theology are as much opposed to various other "neo-orthodox" theologians as they are to liberalism and fundamentalism. Nevertheless, we will follow Gary Dorrien's argument for at least a historical classification of Barth as neo-orthodox: *The Barthian Revolt in Modern Theology* (Louisville, Ky.: Westminster John Knox, 2000), pp. 6-13.

Karl Barth

Karl Barth was born in 1886 in Basel, Switzerland. He studied theology under some of the leading liberal Protestant thinkers of Europe, including Adolf von Harnack, and became a minister of the Reformed Church, first in Geneva and then in the small town of Safenwil on Switzerland's border with Germany. According to his later memoirs, Barth found that the liberal theology of his education did not translate into meaningful preaching that connected with the lives of the average people of the parish. He became disillusioned with liberal Protestantism when his own theological mentors such as Harnack and other German professors publicly supported the Kaiser's war policy in 1914. So the young pastor delved into that perennial source of theological renewal, the apostle Paul's epistle to the Romans, and published *Der Römerbrief* in 1919. In that theological commentary Barth set forth the basic precepts of the neo-orthodox program of dialectical theology or "the theology of the Word of God." The basic thesis is expressed in a separately published essay titled "The Strange New World Within the Bible": "It is not the right human thoughts about God which form the content of the Bible, but the right divine thoughts about men."[6]

Barth was invited to teach theology in Germany after World War I. While teaching at Bonn, he began his great life's project of writing a complete system of theology based on God's Word with the title *Church Dogmatics*. When he died in 1968, it was unfinished at thirteen massive volumes. Barth intended to write a systematic theology completely free of any overpowering philosophical influences and based purely on exegesis of God's Word in Jesus Christ as witnessed to in Scripture. Unlike most other systems of theology—whether liberal or conserva-

---

[6]Karl Barth, *The Word of God and the Word of Man*, trans. Douglas Horton (Boston: Pilgrim, 1928), p. 43.

tive, Protestant or Catholic—*Church Dogmatics* has no prologomena, or foundational section on natural theology or rational evidences for belief in God and Holy Scripture. Instead, Barth launched directly into an exposition of the Word of God in Jesus Christ, the church and Scripture—that is, special revelation. His basic axiom was "The possibility of knowledge of God lies in God's Word and nowhere else."[7] Since Barth considered Jesus Christ to be God's Word in person and therefore identical with God's Word, he asserted that "the eternal God is to be known in Jesus Christ and not elsewhere."[8] Barth eschewed natural theology, philosophical defenses of divine revelation, rational apologetics and any other possible foundation for Christian knowledge of God outside of the self-authenticating gospel of Jesus Christ itself.

While teaching at Bonn, Barth began aiding the anti-Nazi church in Germany, and he refused to pledge loyalty to Hitler and the Nazi Party. He was expelled from Germany by the National Socialist government and took a position as professor of theology at the University of Basel. He remained there until his retirement and death.

Barth was always something of an enigma to his contemporaries. He was the bane of liberal theology's existence—an archconservative with world-class intellectual credentials. To conservatives and especially fundamentalists, he was a wolf in sheep's clothing—a liberal masquerading as a Bible-believing, Jesus-loving Christian. Neither side could make much sense of him, and in their writings they often distorted his theology out of recognition.

One story from near the end of Barth's career reveals much about his personal Christian life. In the early 1960s he made

---

[7] Karl Barth, *Church Dogmatics* 1/1, *The Doctrine of the Word of God*, pt. 1, trans. G. W. Bromiley (Edinburgh, U.K.: T & T Clark, 1975), p. 222.
[8] Karl Barth, *Church Dogmatics* 2/2, *The Doctrine of God*, pt. 2, trans. G. W. Bromiley et al. (Edinburgh, U.K.: T & T Clark, 1957), pp. 191-92.

his only trip to the United States and stopped at the University of Chicago's Rockefeller Chapel, an enormous Gothic cathedral, for a panel conversation with several American theologians. During the question-and-answer time after the panel discussion, a young student stood and asked a question that drew a gasp from the audience: "Professor Barth, could you please summarize your entire life's work in a few words?" Barth is said to have paused only momentarily and then replied, "Yes. In the words of a song my mother taught me when I was a child: 'Jesus loves me, this I know, for the Bible tells me so.'"

An appreciation of Barth's theology must begin with Barth's early observations that the Word of God is threefold: it is the Word become flesh in Jesus Christ, the recorded Word of Scripture, and the proclaimed Word of the church. And what is this threefold Word, this divine revelation to humanity? The Word of God, or divine revelation, is God communicating himself to humanity in his speech. *Deus dixit*—God speaks. God speaks himself. God's Word *is* God himself communicating—not something like information or an experience, but himself. In its most proper sense, then, divine revelation is the event of God's self-communication, and that can only be in Jesus Christ and the prehistory and posthistory of his incarnation.

For Barth, then, Jesus Christ is God's Word. The gospel is Jesus Christ. Jesus Christ is God's revelation. When Barth identifies divine revelation with Jesus Christ, he is not referring to Jesus' teachings or example. He is referring to the person of Jesus Christ in time and eternity. To know Jesus Christ (with or without knowing his human name) is to know God, and one cannot know God without knowing Jesus Christ. Barth did not say that it is impossible to know God without knowing about the Jewish Messiah, who was born in Palestine and died there in about A.D. 30. He was and is the Lord, but his human life on earth does not exhaust his divine-human reality. Barth's view of divine revelation is that Jesus Christ, the Son of God, is God's perfect and complete self-expression, and whatever other authentic revelations of God there may be center on him as promise, hope and memory.

The Bible is not God's Word in the same sense that Jesus Christ is. Jesus Christ is God's Word because he is God himself in action and communication. He shares in God's very being. The Bible is one form of God's Word, and a secondary form at that. Without compromising his high view of Scripture, Barth opposed the fundamentalist Protestant view of the Bible as primary revelation in propositional form. He rejected propositional revelation—the idea that when God wishes to communicate to humans, he communicates information in truth statements. He especially rejected the idea of biblical inerrancy. The Bible, in Barth's understanding, is human through and through. It is a book of human testimony to Jesus Christ, and in spite of all its humanness it is unique because God uses it. According to Barth, the statements of the Bible can be wrong at any point. That does not matter. God has always used fallible and even sinful witnesses, and the Bible is just such a witness. In spite of strong rejection of the orthodox Protestant doctrine of verbal inspiration and especially of inerrancy, Barth held the Bible in high esteem. His denials were not meant to demean the Bible but to elevate Jesus Christ above it. Jesus is Lord! Scripture is not. It is a witness to the Lord.

Barth recognized a third form of divine revelation: the proclamation of the church. The church's proclamation is tertiary—third in priority after Jesus Christ and Scripture. But it can be a means of divine revelation. In and through the preaching and teaching of the church, God sometimes speaks and draws people into encounter with himself. That is not to say that every sermon or service of worship or catechism class is an event of God's Word. It may or may not be. That is Barth's "actualism"—the idea that God reveals himself in acts of self-disclosure. God's Word of "divine revelation" is never an object to be possessed. It cannot be manipulated or owned. It happens. It has happened in Jesus Christ. It happens through Scripture. It may happen in the church's proclamation and teaching. Jesus Christ is Lord of Scripture and the church. Scripture is the authority in the church because it is the primary witness to Jesus Christ. The church is the context for divine-human encounter in which Scripture is expounded and Jesus proclaimed. All of this is divine revelation. But it all centers on Jesus Christ.

By highlighting these three means of the Word of God, Barth is not trying to limit God or lock God into revealing God's self in certain occasions or locations to the exclusion of others. Instead, what is being affirmed is the overwhelming generosity of God's revelation: God is faithful to meet us, desires to meet us, and will meet us through Scripture and proclamation.

While many other themes of Barth's theology should be discussed, we have focused exclusively on his doctrine of revelation, the Word of God, because the linchpin of neo-orthodoxy lies in its concept of divine revelation. Revelation proper is God's special self-disclosure in events and above all in Jesus Christ. God reveals *himself,* not propositional statements. God reveals himself *specially,* not in vague, universal human experiences (Schleiermacher's *Gefühl*) or nature or universal history. For neo-orthodox Protestant theologians, God's revelation comes as an invasion into human history and experience and is never identical with the results of "man's search for God" or even the words and propositions of Scripture.

Common Neo-orthodox Themes

Barth was certainly the key formulator of this new trajectory in theology, what scholars now call neo-orthodoxy, but he was not the only voice. Other Protestant and a few Catholic theologians joined in his reformation of modern theology, adding their own twists to it, including Emil Brunner (1889-1966) and Rein-

hold Niebuhr (1893-1971). While Brunner and Niebuhr both
vehemently disagreed with Barth on a number of key points,
they can still be identified as neo-orthodox in at least three
senses. First, all three (with the possible exception of Niebuhr)
are thoroughly christocentric. That is, they see Jesus Christ as
the revelation of God in person and seek to center everything
in their theological reflections on him. To the neo-orthodox
theologians, Jesus Christ is more than a prophet of history and
more even than a fully God-conscious man. He is God's Son
breaking into the world of nature and history from beyond.

Second, all of the neo-orthodox theologians reject natural
theology (which explores what humans can know about God
prior to special revelation) and embrace God's Word as source
and norm for Christian theology. They all refuse to identify
God's "Word" with the words and propositions of Scripture. Yet
they hold the Bible in high regard as the special witness to and
instrument of God's Word. In neo-orthodoxy the Bible is neither merely a great book of human religious wisdom (as in
much liberal theology) nor "that manuscript from heaven" (as
in fundamentalism). It is a thoroughly human book with all the
marks and characteristics of the human authors. It is historical,
fallible and culturally conditioned at every point. On the other
hand, it is the unique channel of God's Word and becomes
God's Word in the moment that God chooses to use it to bring
people into encounter with himself.

Finally, all of the neo-orthodox theologians emphasize
what Søren Kierkegaard called the infinite qualitative difference between time and eternity. That includes the "wholly oth-
erness" of God and God's kingdom. It implies also the
paradoxical nature of human formulations about God arising
out of reflection on God's Word. No human social order or
organization, including the church, can be identified with
God's kingdom. No ideology or philosophy, including theological systems, can be exclusively identified with God's own truth.

CONTEMPORARY THEOLOGY STRUGGLES WITH DIVERSITY

Anyone who has ever read a nineteenth-century Russian novel has probably experienced the same confusion that most people feel on first glimpse at the wide and disarrayed variety of late-twentieth-century theologies. What has happened to the plot? Who are all these characters? Post-World War II Christian theology is diverse as never before. Especially since the culturally revolutionary 1960s, the story of Christian theology has taken so many dizzying twists and turns and splintered in so many new directions that even experts find it difficult to draw it all together into one coherent story. What makes it all "Christian"? Where is the thread that is supposed to tie it all together as one story line? A quick glance at some of the adjectives now affixed to the word *theology* give a hint of the growing diversity: *postliberal, liberation, postmodern, death-of-God, process, narrative, postcolonial, feminist, womanist, ecotheological, black, radically orthodox, paleoorthodox, open, evangelical, correlational.* At the risk of doing injustice to the rich diversity of theologies now emerging, we will highlight only two movements.

Evangelical Theology

As fundamentalists became more and more sectarian and narrow in the 1940s and 1950s, many conservative Protestants wanted to distance themselves from that movement while remaining theologically orthodox. Several issues divided those conservative Protestants who wished to be called evangelicals from those who were fundamentalists. Their areas of agreement were significant as well. Both fundamentalists and the new evangelicals emphasized the supernatural inspiration of the Bible, the major doctrinal achievements of the early Christian church, such as the Nicene Creed, and Protestant orthodoxy. These closely related movements both emphasized conversional piety as a hallmark of authentic Christianity and rejected baptismal regeneration as well as universalism. The new evangelicals rejected what they saw as fundamentalism's divisiveness over relatively minor doctrinal and moral issues and wished to develop and nurture a broader coalition of conservative, conversional Protestant Christianity. For them, biblical inspiration implied scriptural infallibility but not necessarily absolute technical accuracy of every detail recorded in the biblical literature. Nor did it require a literalistic hermeneutic, especially with regard to origins and the end times. The new evangelicals insisted on God as Creator of everything *(creatio ex nihilo)* and the second coming of Jesus Christ in the future, but they allowed great variation of interpretation regarding the details of these doctrines.

The doctrinal freedom within evangelicalism eventually led to tensions. At one end of the spectrum, the more conservative evangelicals promoted a return to the roots of fundamentalist doctrine, while experiential evangelicals, at the other end of the spectrum, promoted evangelism, conversion and spirituality. Conservative evangelicals feared that this focus on Christian experience could lead their coalition partners into liberalism. Experientialist evangelicals—equally committed to biblical authority and historic Christian doctrines—criticized their suspicious orthodox coalition partners for failing to shed entirely the fundamentalist mentality and for one-sidedly emphasizing the doctrinal content of Christianity to the neglect of experience of the living God. Tensions developed and grew between these two wings of the post-World War II evangelical coalition, so that by the late 1980s and early 1990s they were sparring with one another over which one represented true evangelicalism.

What do the various versions of evangelical theology have in common? Adherents of the two paradigms share commitment to a basic historic Christian worldview, including belief in God's transcendence and supernatural activity, the Bible as divinely inspired and infallible in matters of faith and practice, Jesus Christ as crucified and risen Savior and Lord of the world, conversion as the only authentic initiation into salvation, and evangelism through communication of the gospel to all people. They also reject liberal theology and fundamentalism to varying degrees. Evangelicals have been ambivalent about Karl Barth and neo-orthodoxy. Those closest to the fundamentalist roots of the movement sternly reject them, while those furthest away from fundamentalism see them as friends and allies.

Liberation Theologies

Throughout the 1970s groups of socially, economically and politically oppressed Christians in North and South America began to develop theologies of liberation. North American black theologians focused their attention on the problem of racism and interpreted salvation as including the liberation of African Americans from racial prejudice and exclusion. Some of the leading black theologians of the 1970s went so far as to suggest that God is black and that salvation in the modern North American context means "becoming black with God." These enigmatic statements should not be taken too literally. The point James Cone and others were making is that God is on the side of the oppressed and downtrodden and that people seeking salvation cannot remain neutral in the situation of racial division and oppression. In Latin America, both Catholic and Protestant theologians began reflecting theologically on that continent's situation of extreme poverty and economic injustice and interpreted salvation as including abolition of structural poverty and unjust political orders. Throughout the 1980s, North American feminist theologians increasingly focused attention on the problem of sexism and patriarchy in both church and society. They interpreted salvation as including equality of men and women and even radical readjustment of not only male domination but all political-social hierarchies.

Liberation theologians of all kinds reject a universal theology that is for all people everywhere. Each oppressed group must have the freedom to reflect critically on Scripture and the situation in which they live and to decide for itself how best to interpret and live out the gospel message. For liberation theologies of all kinds, theology is concrete, committed reflection on praxis in the light of God's Word. *Praxis* means "liberating activity" and is what happens in any situation of oppression when people begin to free themselves and seek equality and justice. The theologian's task is to help the people in their struggle for liberation by linking it with God's Word.

Further, liberation theologians insist that God has a preferential option for the oppressed and the oppressed have special insight into God's will in any given social situation. This does not mean that African Americans or women or the poor have an automatically favorable relationship with God that gives them an advantage in being saved. Liberation theologians tend to think of "salvation" mainly in historical and social ways rather than individualistically. They believe that God takes sides with oppressed people and actively seeks to liberate them from all bondage, slavery and inequality. When one group is being oppressed by another such that its people are being hindered from the fulfillment of their potential, God sides with the oppressed group in its active struggle to liberate itself and to achieve full humanity for its members.

Three key liberation theologians need to be mentioned. James Cone (b. 1938) is often considered the father of African American theology. In the late 1960s and early 1970s he became closely associated with the Black Power movement of Malcolm X and other African Americans who were dissatisfied with Martin Luther King Jr.'s pacifist approach to combating racism. Cone wrote two groundbreaking and highly controversial theological volumes that justify radical activism: *Black Theology and Black Power* (1969) and *A Black Theology of Liberation*

(1970). He argued that God is black and that black power is "Christ's central message to twentieth-century America,"[9] and he seemed to condone if not actually advocate race war if that was what it would take to abolish racism in the United States. Cone became Charles H. Briggs Professor of Systematic Theology at the prestigious and liberal Union Theological Seminary in the 1970s. He continued to develop black theology based on African American experience of oppression and liberation in numerous books and articles. Critics consider him a dangerously radical and divisive voice in contemporary Christian theology, while sympathizers see him as a prophet like Amos in the Old Testament.

The father of Latin American liberation theology is Gustavo Gutiérrez (b. 1928), who lives in Lima, Peru, and whose book *A Theology of Liberation* (1971) is still that movement's basic text. Gutiérrez is a Catholic theologian with wide ecumenical contacts. He travels frequently to North America and Europe to spread the message of liberation theology and to engage in frank discussions with theologians of affluent countries. He has identified the root causes of Latin American political and economic injustice with North American and European manipulation and interference through his "dependency theory." According to the Peruvian theologian, Latin American economic dependency on North American and European economies and governments is purposely structured to benefit those already affluent societies and keep Southern Hemisphere societies and cultures underprivileged. Like many other liberation theologians, most of whom look to him as their spokesman and leader, Gutiérrez sees salvation as the overthrow of those forces that keep Latin America majorities poor and the subsequent establishment of economic democ-

---

[9]James H. Cone, *Black Theology and Black Power* (New York: Seabury, 1969), p. 1.

racies that are basically socialistic if not communistic in nature. He looks to the economic and political theories of Karl Marx for inspiration and guidance, while rejecting Marx's atheism and materialism.

The leading voice in feminist theology is Rosemary Radford Ruether (b. 1936), author of one of the movement's major texts, *Sexism and God-Talk* (1983). Together with other feminist Christians, Ruether, a Catholic theologian who teaches at a Methodist seminary, argues that patriarchy is a basic evil that needs to be abolished in order for salvation to be accomplished. By *patriarchy* she means not just male domination—although that is the literal meaning of the term—but the entire hierarchical structure of society put in place by both men and women in which father figures control everything. Even God ought not to be conceived as an all-controlling being above everyone else. According to Ruether, God ought to be called "God/dess" and conceived as the "matrix of being" that connects everyone and everything together in a web of equality and interrelatedness. Because women are closer to being attuned to such a vision of society, Ruether advocates the establishment of "Women-Churches" as alternative communities to male-dominated denominations and congregations. Such Women-Churches will be safe places for feminists (including males with feminized consciousness) to explore the new paradigm of feminist theology in teaching and liturgy centered entirely on women's experiences.

CONCLUSION

Here ends our story. But there is much story yet to be told. Fresh storytellers are continually writing new dramatic scenes and rediscovering old ones. Unlike the traditional Shakespearean five-act play, the Christian story will not end with the conclusion of the fifth act; the curtains of a new millennium are even now being pulled back on a new drama of faith. With roughly two billion adherents to Christianity, most of whom do not live in the United States or Europe, we should not be surprised to find the next major act of Christian theology being played out on a non-Western stage by non–Anglo-Saxons.

Index